Lying, Cheating and Stealing

Using and Abusing the Corporate System for Personal Gain

By E. D. Everett

ISBN-10: 0-9860323-1-X
ISBN-13: 978-0-9860323-1-8

This work requires a two-fold dedication. First, to my coworkers over the years who knew something was wrong but were afraid to come forward and, second, to my beautiful wife without whose encouragement and expertise the creative urge would likely have foundered.

E. D. Everett

At your place of employment:

- Do you think hard work pays off?
- Do you think loyalty to the company is rewarded?
- Do you think integrity is a valued asset?
- Do you think back-room deals are a thing of the past?
- Do you think your HR department is working for the best interests of the employees?
- Do you think your boss takes note of your extra effort?
- Do you expect raises based on how well you do your job?

If you answered "Yes" to any of these questions, read on to learn about the unfortunate reality in modern corporate America.

E. D. Everett

Introduction

The situations, attitudes, procedures and incidents in this book have all been taken from my personal experiences in life, in business.

To fully appreciate the content, the reader must be the type of person who believes a successful career in a corporate business environment is directly proportional to hard work, talent and ethics. It is to this person that this book is directed. You poor sucker. You couldn't be more mistaken!

There are many people, successful people, who look at a business not with an eye toward how they can use their business acumen or technical expertise to advance company goals, increase productivity or enhance efficiency, but with an eye toward how easily they can infiltrate the halls of power, use the system to their advantage and extract from this corporate victim as much *personal* success as possible.

Unique but universal

Basing a themed book on personal experience is hazardous since any one person's perspective will be at once limited and unique. My observations nevertheless will strike a chord with workers in many fields and many organizations. The reason is simple: People are people and have always been so and will always be so. And their motivations—good or bad—haven't changed one iota over time. A reading of Homer's classics, Gibbons' Decline and Fall, Tolstoy and others will confirm this statement as true, at least for western civilization, and I would place a heavy bet that this conclusion is universally true.

My descriptions will, however, imperfectly apply to many organizations, especially those businesses that tend toward smaller operations, such as the family-owned-and-run concern, the business unit that is overseen or directly influenced by an entrepreneur, and start-ups. While instances of bad behavior still occur in these environments, in my view they are less likely.

The reasons for this imperfection are again straightforward. The scenarios described here are prevalent where there are several layers of management, perhaps several divisions within an organization, and multiple locations involved. This complexity is missing in a mom and pop operation. A level of anonymity and corporate insulation is necessary to wring maximum personal success from a modern business in the U.S.

In an entrepreneurial scenario, the business is often run by a dynamic person or tightly-knit group with an idea for a service or product they are passionate about. In this case, it is common for the leader(s) to take a hands-on approach, whether handling the largest or smallest details. He will seek out and hire people having the same passion for the product or service, while avoiding or eliminating those who don't. Here, you must be on board and pulling hard in the same direction as your executive and his core team, or you will be gone.

In a start-up, it's all about survival in the first critical years. For the business to succeed there is no room for waste, period. The books will be looked at closely for sales vs. revenue, margins, EBIT and all the rest. Any expenditures that can be cut or appear excessive will stand out, and will be the focus of attention sooner or later. Any person not contributing to the overall success of the endeavor will likewise be the focus of critical attention.

What is success?

Success, in the context of this book, is defined as the achievement of *personal* goals and is in no direct way related to the success of the business or organization itself. This is the main mind-set hurdle that has to be overcome by the naïve to understand the thinking that permeates corporate culture today, and so we repeat: One need not be concerned with whether the business succeeds or fails. Of course, it's better if it succeeds as this means more money in the pot so to speak, and success keeps the proverbial Golden Goose alive, but there is a great deal of personal success that can be gotten out of businesses that are limping along or failing. Those innocent persons who go to work each day trying to maximize effort in the direction of saving the company money or maximizing profit; those who come up with some technique or process or gizmo that will pay off financially for the organization—these people are wasting precious resources that could be better used for personal gain. In addition, this traditional ethical behavior leaves the playing field open for those who *do* know how to work the system. Moreover, I would add that the ones playing the system are *counting on* those who to come in to work each day and do the right thing. By doing so they help to keep the system going, the goose alive.

I was once asked if personal goals may not coincide with company goals producing a win-win scenario. Yes, they may, and this is just the case with good, honest, ethical employees. These employees are not, however, the ones we are speaking of here. We are describing those whose goals run counter to the company's and for whom these goals are a target for personal success.

Success for some may consist only of remuneration but for others it may not include a financial component at all. Success becomes a unique personal objective that may include money but also can include other measures and symbols of "success" such as power, influence, control, recognition, empire-building, prestige, security, perks and perhaps other darker goals. Having said that, I believe it is true that the goal of transferring, by whatever means, the maximum amount of money from the company's bank account into one's personal account explains the actions of most "successful" workers and managers. To be clear, by "transfer" I am not referring to white-collar crime such as embezzlement but to the apparently legitimate vehicles of salary, commissions, bonuses and perks. There is certainly a heavy dose of unethical and sometimes even immoral behavior, but generally not blatant crime. Some may decide to step over the line into illegality, but why, when there is an open field of opportunity just this side of the line?

What company are we talking about?

When referring to "the company," the "organization" or "the management," I am drawing from a lifetime of work experience with a small number of companies primarily involved in the automotive, aerospace and medical industries.

One of my short term positions was as a unionized blue collar worker on the production line of one of the "Big 3" U.S. auto manufacturers, although the thrust of this book is not aimed at or derived from a union environment. The problems with productivity, efficiency, cost control and such at unionized plants are beyond the scope of this work and I'm sure are covered by any number of volumes. It is enough to say that the organized us-against-them adversarial attitudes in these plants sufficiently distort the employee-management relationship as to make it almost unrecognizable.

(For the union worker, some of the questionable practices described herein are simply not an option; those in the union management and those on the "other side" —the white collar side— have more opportunities for abuse. But I would say in general that the kind of abuse I describe in the following sections is less prevalent in union shops than in non-union workplaces for a number of reasons. Since the unions are essentially continuously striking or threatening to strike for more money, more benefits, less work, guaranteed jobs, more time off, or posturing, making demands, writing grievances, executing costly and inefficient contracts for endless training, and promoting the despicably wrong-headed seniority system, the unionized company has a narrower profit margin than it otherwise would. In other words, there is less to plunder for personal "success." In many cases, unionized plants must struggle just to avoid bankruptcy after meeting, or trying to meet, union demands.)

In my view, the reduced profit margins and more structured hierarchy in unionized plants make them a less attractive target for those who want to play the system. Even so, human nature dictates that we should expect to find bad behavior cropping up but perhaps in different ways and with different dimensions than in a non-union environment.

Organizational structure

To provide a coherent framework upon which to hang the descriptions that follow, I will create a fictional business, a distillation of the sum total of places and people I have worked with and for.

Our amalgamated company is one with more than 5,000 employees, is international, has multiple product divisions, uses internal and external distributor and dealer salesmen to reach and support customers, and also uses business partners (independent businesses with special standing) for technical support of end users.

The products are generally quite technical, requiring operator training, factory installers and calibration personnel. Middle management includes sales, technical, software and product managers. A significant portion of revenue is diverted to R&D such that new products are introduced on a regular basis keeping our composite company at or near the leading edge in its field.

Manufacturing is done in several locations around the world. Training and support are supplied to satellite businesses and the end users, and so a significant number of employees are traveling at any given time.

My position

Although part of the sales department for a significant portion of my career, my background is technical and I have worked several years in non-sales positions and in field service. Compensation has generally been via salary, but some compensation, earlier in my career, was hourly; sometimes with a yearly performance contract, sometimes not. As part of the sales department, I sometimes had commission incentives, sometimes not.

Let's assume, for the purposes of this work, that my location is a small operation relative to the overall size of the company, but not the smallest. It has some manufacturing capability, but is not responsible for the main production of the business.

I had a chance to work with customers, existing and potential, and at various times have worked for and with managers from our division president and VPs down to middle managers. I have been fortunate to travel and work with international managers and technical personnel from across the world too.

My purpose

I have been dismayed and sometimes shocked by the behavior of so-called respectable and intelligent managers and have considered the reasons: Is it me? Is it bad luck? In talking to fellow employees, I have heard numerous stories about similar experiences. Why? Could it be them, their bad luck, or what? What makes this experience so common?

I have been stubborn and have resisted accepting this behavior as normal, desirable or profitable to any company. It ultimately is damaging as it tends to drive away good people who won't put up with it, and lowers the morale of those who remain behind. But still the question, why? The answer has to be that the less-than-professional behavior pays off—not for the company, but for the individual bad actor himself. For him,[1] personal goals outweigh company goals. Basic compensation is not enough; he has to have more power, influence, control—whatever defines success in his eyes.

My purpose in writing this book, aside from enjoying the cathartic effect, is to set down specific experiences such that others suffering through their careers will see that they are not alone, that this distorted management style, while prevalent, is *not* right and hopefully elucidate the reasons why it "works."

---

[1] Throughout most of this work I have used masculine pronouns instead of the tedious he/she, him/her format.

My purpose is *not* to point out the flaws of individuals. As mentioned above, human flaws are well known and extensively documented. No, the aim is to expose unprofessional practices, their consequences and manifestations in corporate America.

Format

This work consists of independent chapters, in a more or less random order, that are each self-contained units. Some, such as the first segment on communication, have a general relevance to many aspects of business life while others relate to specific areas of concern or abuse.

Each section begins with a statement or statements that could have been taken out of some "Management's Guide to Ethical Business Practices" or a "Corporate Policy Manual" publication.

Following that, a dose of reality provides a stark contrast to the common-sense policy statement. I have tried to include at least one real-world example from my experience to illustrate the consequences of each of these policy distortions.

Each chapter concludes with a description of why this corruption of policy works and what the reward might be to the perpetrator.

E. D. Everett

Talk to Me

Communication is a requirement for efficient operation and positive employee morale. It includes clear communication of the current status of corporate directives, policies and goals. It also includes performance feedback to employees, facilitating continuous improvement.

Wrong!

When management has been infiltrated by one or more well-placed players using the system for their personal gain, open communication is perhaps the single most disruptive business practice in their eyes. It has to be avoided at all costs at the very same time that management gives vociferous lip service in favor of it.

Why would this be so? When anyone in upper management is involved in achieving goals not in line the corporate vision, not in compliance with stated corporate policy (i.e. personal goals) it of course behooves them to keep this truth hidden. At the same time, the appearance of open and forthright communication must be preserved to camouflage their true objectives.

The contradiction of blocking communication while promoting it is implemented by having phony programs such as suggestion plans, brain storming sessions, corporate initiatives and the like all ostensibly in support of and encouraging ever-increasing communication. Management will continue to believably express their dismay at the lack of sufficient communication, express regret that, yes, even the top managers are guilty, and pledge to correct this situation immediately. The *faux* correction plans may involve management meetings to expose and rectify faulty attitudes along with a call for frequent and regular meetings with lower level employees.[2]

In this communication improvement campaign, it will be emphasized that the dialog is bi-directional and must flow downwards and upwards. It is expected that even those at the lowest level in the organization contribute to information flow.

In this way the status quo prevails, hidden behind a flurry of meaningless activity. I have personally seen any number of these programs come and go and have marveled at their transparent ineffectiveness.

It is interesting to note that continuing to clamp down on official meaningful communication while at the same time encouraging the lower levels to speak up creates a handy one-way transfer of information to management. This upward-directed pipeline can be useful to gauge the mood and reaction of the workers and can be used as an indicator of how well or poorly the initiatives are being received.

Why This Works

It works because the general employee, the one playing by traditional rules, recognizes there is a communication problem, is relieved to hear management acknowledge it, and is excited to see that something, at last, will be done about it. While the last round of initiatives for this same purpose proved ineffective, this time it will surely be better. Any incremental improvement will be welcome and so the employee looks forward hopefully to the future.

A significant number of employees will embrace the proposed actions and will thereby be pacified, for the time being, by the

---

[2] The impact of the fact that these activities give the management team a purpose, an appearance of serious activity, and an abundantly full calendar cannot be overstated. One of the main incidental benefits of management inventing "problems" to "correct" is that the self-imposed activities give them something to do. When you have a competent work force in place, fully trained and experienced, it is amazing how few managers it takes to "run" an organization.

"progress" being made. It remains for the long-term employee to reflect on the fact that none of the initiatives, plans, meetings, speeches or pledges from the several past iterations of communication improvement strategies seem to have worked.

So it is that the appearance of substantive action continually masks the real goal: To keep the communication channels tightly controlled for the private use of those admitted to the privileged group.

The Payoff

The maxim that "knowledge is power" applies here. As you may imagine, there is more than one benefit to tightly controlling communication. Keeping the knowledge of questionable or shady dealings limited to as few as possible protects the guilty from exposure. Keeping the truth of a manager's real plans and goals hidden allows him to proceed unimpeded, at least for a time.

E. D. Everett

Shoot the Messenger

Management should encourage feedback from the lowest levels regarding issues requiring management attention for the betterment of business practices, employee relations, or any other aspect of the corporate system. Management should loudly proclaim an "open door" policy and repeatedly solicit any and all persons to express their concerns either in a group setting or in confidential privacy, as appropriate.

Get a clue...

Management has no interest in improving (read: changing) the status quo *unless* it will positively affect their personal goals. They are only interested in input that may be useful in that regard now or in the future.

In my experience, input from the lower levels is generally a genuine attempt by a worker to rectify a procedure, an inequity, or raise some other legitimate concern. Now, this input may incidentally touch upon or expose one or more of the failings or questionable practices of the current powers-that-be and, as such, must be cut off firmly and forcefully.

A common way to nip it in the bud is to immediately and in no uncertain terms put the employee on the defensive as soon as he expresses the offending comment. This is such a common practice that I sometimes wonder if it is taught in business management courses, although it seems more likely that such behavior is a natural reaction by someone who feels threatened by an inferior.

Why This Works

In my effort to be a conscientious employee, I once sent an email to my boss with time-sensitive information contained therein. As is my routine with important correspondence, I sent the email with a return receipt request. After receiving the receipt notification, and after allowing time for the email contents to be digested, I knocked on the boss' door.

"I see you read my email. Is it too early to discuss?"

"How do you know I read the email?"

"I sent it with a receipt request."

Silence.

"That way, I know if an important email has been received."

Silence and then, "Why in the world would you do that?"

Now it was my turn to be silent as I thought:

- a) that I had just answered that question,
- b) that even without an answer the reason for such a tool is clear and,
- c) why *not* use such tools as are available when appropriate?

The thought then crossed my mind, "Does he, a vice president, not know of this tool?"

"Um, you know, like you would do through the U.S. Mail with important papers for which you want confirmation of receipt."

Silence.

There is an aside here worthy of note. It is incumbent on a manager to never, ever, answer a direct question from an underling in a serious and forthright way as this puts the manager on the defensive which is, for him, an unacceptable position. Answering has the following negative aspects, from the manager's viewpoint:

- It shifts control of the conversation to the underling;
- It may expose the fact that the manager may not have an answer;
- It may cause the manager to have to think and decide the issue extemporaneously, a clear opportunity to misspeak or blunder;
- It causes the issue in question to appear to be debatable or negotiable in some way, which it likely is not.

Anyway, back to the email conversation, which we left at a moment of silence. By this point in the conversation management's goal has been achieved. The original question has not been answered, no feedback has been given relating to the email content, and the employee is now on the defensive trying to explain the use of a software tool, the reason for use of which is clear, the existence of which the manager is aware, or should be.

Also by this time, the employee's mind-set has shifted. Has he just embarrassed the boss by exposing his ignorance? Has he just made a *faux pas* and, if so, how to recover? Perhaps the email response is not so important right now after all.

This last thought is not to be minimized. With an "open door" policy, the underling is generally, as in the above example, speaking to someone with the power to hire and fire. Even when not explicit, the threat of firing is always there.

And there we have the essence and beauty of the "open door" policy. Sure, come and talk to me anytime. Bring your complaints, comments and questions. By the way, remember, I can fire you.

The Payoff

Eliminating questions and squelching dissent, keeping the workers intimidated, and clearing the way for one to continue a management style without fear of having to answer to employees or to explain one's actions—need we say more?

Management by Intimidation

Management should be even-handed in its dealings with employees, both respecting good, long term workers, while at the same time dealing fairly but decisively with those violating company policy.

Don't go there...

As mentioned elsewhere, management must at all times keep in control of communication, keep control during meetings, and always keep the upper hand when dealing one-on-one with employees. Each of these techniques is a sometimes not-so-subtle message of intimidation to the worker.

It is not uncommon for management, however, to blatantly intimidate employees into being submissive and compliant. One striking event comes to mind. When our service teams were consolidated from four zones across the continental U.S. to three, several states and their respective service areas were shifted into one of the three larger zones. We in the Midwest had to learn the management style of the New York team and they were keen to demonstrate their power. Their solution? They summarily fired the most senior service engineer from each area. These were men of 10+ years of experience who, until the consolidation, were well respected and each carried their weight in their respective areas.

Note that the zone consolidation was a reduction in *management*, not in the number of customers to be supported, so the elimination of a group of key field individuals hurt our *customers* most in the following ways: 1) each area lost a key representative with a great deal of knowledge and experience, one who had developed a rapport with most, if not all, of the important customers in his area; 2) response time got longer since we had fewer experienced people to respond to calls; 3) newbies hired to fill the gap take between six months to a year to become competent on their own; and 4) the remaining employees' morale took a precipitous drop.

Why This Works

For management, this works because they now have every remaining employee's attention. At the same time they have lowered their payroll costs since the most senior workers are typically receiving the highest compensation.

For employees who have an alternative employment option, it may *not* work because they could opt to leave and go elsewhere in the hopes of a more stable environment. For those who don't have an option, it works just fine as they will likely shut up and get to work as they know that they could be fired at any time for no reason. It's not surprising that morale took a nosedive.

The Payoff

It is rare to find a worker who relishes the thought of changing jobs and for would-be managers this fact is extremely useful. It only takes the slightest hint such as a memo or statement that includes "...in times of high unemployment..." to remind a worker that it may be best to keep his head down and get to work. The manager who does not have the skill or ability to lead using positive reinforcements may be happy to fall back on this sort of intimidation.

It's hard to imagine the thought processes that occur in the minds of managers who would stoop to this sort of tactic. One has to believe that they don't understand the value of experience. They must also not comprehend that, as mentioned, this move didn't help their cause in any way but instead hurt everyone involved: The company, our customers, the terminated employees, and the management team in particular.

A move like this, implemented to teach respect, and to show the workers who's boss, exactly backfired. We in the field lost all respect for the leadership, and trusted them not at all to make good decisions with rational motives.

E. D. Everett

Here's an Idea

No one knows the details of a job better than someone who works at it day after day. A forward thinking organization will seek out and reward employees for good ideas that save the company money, improve efficiency or increase the value of our hardware, software and services to our customers.

What a day for a daydream...

A suggestion plan can be used for a number of purposes. One is to get employees to come up with ideas for improvement, another is to find out who's complaining about what, another might be to pick and choose among the ideas presented in order to make sure the "right" people are rewarded with a cash award proportional to the savings or value assigned to the suggestion by the review committee.

In working amongst both the technical and sales personnel, we had the opportunity to advance several ideas through the company suggestion program. One top notch software developer whom I know and have a good relationship with had a suggestion rejected only to see his exact suggestion implemented a few months later— no mention of his idea and certainly no reward. He opted out of the suggestion program from that point forward.

I had a similar experience. Because I spent a good deal of time out of the office at customers within driving distance, a set of circumstances generated what I thought was a no-lose idea for the company. When using our company car, we paid for fuel and maintenance via an expense account. Those without a company car could use their personal vehicle and would be reimbursed for mileage only. When using a rental car, in addition to the rental charges, the employee can expense rental car fuel as well.

Infrequently, when my company car was in the shop or otherwise unavailable, I used a rental car or my personal car. By coincidence, I made two trips to two different customers once using a rental car with unlimited mileage for each customer and once using my personal car for each customer. One was about 300 miles away and the other closer to 600 miles away. In this way I ended up with comparative data for the cost to the company of each trip versus distance and method of transportation.

I didn't think much about this data until I found a copy of a project manager's expense report lying on the copy machine. I returned it to him but couldn't help but notice a mileage reimbursement for his personal car to the tune of 3,600 miles for *one month*! Since none of the project managers have a company car (officers of the company, department managers, salesmen, service technicians, and few others are allotted cars) I could only imagine what their mileage costs might be if they all chose to use a personal vehicle.

So the logical conclusion was for me to submit a suggestion to change our travel policy such that, based on mileage, an employee should consider his personal car for shorter trips and a rental with unlimited mileage for longer ones. I included a small spreadsheet showing the data from my comparative trips indicating the breakpoint based on the current fuel price and mileage reimbursement rate. Simple.

Well, the suggestion was *accepted and rejected at the same time* (Hello 1984!). It was accepted for inclusion in the travel policy but rejected for payment of a reward. When I questioned the awkward decision, I was told that a similar statement was already in the policy regarding the use of the employees' discretion in deciding the most cost effective means of travel.

The two responses discussed here, plus a number of other questionable rejections and awards, caused me also to opt out of the suggestion program from that point forward.

Why This Works

A program such as this works to improve morale while improving the organization only if it is responsibly administered. As employees see it being misused, they opt out and morale drops, not to mention the fact that good ideas are lost because they are not submitted. In our case, we had repeated pleadings from upper management to please use the suggestion program as the number of entries dried up. The program was changed, renamed, rewards were expanded, and still participation flagged.

The Payoff

We know the payoff here is the short term acquisition of ideas from the general employee. Awards can be made or withheld depending on the goals of management. Once the input dries up, meetings can be held to re-shuffle the program parameters and re-launch it. There is, as has been mentioned before, something to be said for a system that keeps managers' schedules full and keeps them appearing busy and engaged.

E. D. Everett

Book-of-the-Month Leadership

A president or CEO must use a balance of good judgment and good advice, noting trends both within his organization and in the business environment, with a view toward legal and ethical ramifications when making decisions about the future direction of the company.

Try again...

If a CEO recognizes his limitations in regards to good judgment and decision-making, he may rely on the wisdom of others to help him steer a course into the future. In the best scenario, he will receive and digest honest, insightful input from his trusted advisors, and formulate a plan with the highest potential for success. At the worst, he will believe any and all persons who present what appears to him to be a credible case for an initiative, and may make decisions that affect the entire organization based on that presentation.

Or, as in my experience, a CEO may get a book for Christmas (such as the ones you've seen prominently displayed in bookstore windows that describe how this or that CEO transformed a company into a world-beater, made billions doing so, and is loved by all of his grateful employees) and base our company's new direction on it. He will buy the whole premise hook, line and sinker, and institute changes, programs and procedures directly taken from the latest best seller.

Why This Works

It doesn't work. Sure, we again have the *appearance* of leadership, but the procedures or changes that worked in some other industry, under different conditions than ours, are generally imperfectly interpreted, incorrectly applied, or applied in a half-hearted manner to "see how it goes." As such, they are ineffective and end up being a burden on the workers who have to adapt to the changes, try to make sense out of them, and struggle to make them work. After a while, and with hardly a whimper, the new initiatives fade away and are mostly forgotten, sometimes before the next Christmas rolls around.

In the end we learned not to get overly excited about the new book and the resulting changes because we knew if we gritted our teeth and held on, the next book would come out and we would start all over with new procedures and yet another new direction.

The Payoff

When flailing for management direction and leadership options, there is some comfort derived from relying on others. By latching onto a well-regarded, successful and published business persona's ideas, a clueless leader believes he can pick from among the best ideas and share in the success of the book's author, while at the same time garner the respect and admiration of his underlings for his cleverness and decisiveness.

This approach requires less work than thinking up new ideas, and it gives the manager a new project with which he can busy himself and his team for the next few months. Do not underestimate the benefits that accrue to a manger who projects the *appearance* of genuine leadership.

Unfortunately for the company, the cost-to-benefit ratio of this type of questionable leadership is immense. Implementing book-of-the-month ideas just to have them replaced again and again may result in the occasional nugget of improvement but in general does not pan out.

The mindset required for this type of management practice continues to puzzle me. It has to feature a short attention span, mental blinders and mild gullibility at the very least. One would have to buy into the new book, consultant recommendation, or business practice fad while at the same time blocking out the previous implementation. And one would have to possess the incredible ability to stand up with a straight face announcing the new direction to his staff that he knows, at least at *some* level, must remember the last episode and the one before that. How one would do this while never mentioning the earlier iteration is a trick that perhaps a psychologist could explain.

E. D. Everett

Take Me to Your Leader

A healthy company has a clear and published organizational chart showing the lines of responsibility from the bottom up to the top. A president or CEO will stand up as the person ultimately responsible, sharing credit for the good and taking blame for the bad.

He is a dynamic leader, a manager of people and ideas, an inspiration to the workers, a shining example that we can follow and from whom we can learn to be the best that we can be.

You've got to be kidding…

In the composite company under discussion we have a president who was promoted over the years from an entry-level position. His educational background is neither managerial nor technical. He does however have a good personality when it suits him, carefully keeping his Mr. Hyde side hidden for the most part, showing it only to inferiors whom he wishes to silence or otherwise intimidate.

It became painfully clear to me after a number of years watching the ever-changing strategy, the new directives, the newer directives countermanding the previous directives, the string of clearly misguided choices for executive-level placements, and much more, that our leader was flailing in his attempt to lead. Once in a while he would hit a home run as you would expect just by sheer luck, but generally the decisions were questionable at best, disastrous at worst.

Why This Works

The way our company is structured could be compared to a car dealership. The main headquarters is elsewhere as is the primary manufacturing site; the primary engineering for our products is done elsewhere as well. Our job at our location is simply to represent the products, sell them, and support them. The products are generally well-designed and so will sell at some level whether we do a good job or a mediocre job. Not least important is the fact that our good company name and reputation brings customers through the door no matter what we do. What must be avoided at all cost is screwing up enough to lose customers or drive them away in sufficient numbers for international headquarters to notice.

Because of this arrangement, there is quite a bit of room for inept management, a buffer zone if you will. It would take a credible report of serious malfeasance or an unexpected drop in revenue reaching the desk of international management before a red flag would be raised. And even then there would be weeks or months before an investigation could be completed—plenty of time for the covering of tracks.

Our leader surrounds himself with advisors, some with greater, some with lesser capability than he, few with any genuine management training or expertise. Unfortunately, being easily influenced, he is prey for those who will manipulate others for their own gain. Those advisors soon recognize that it is to their significant advantage to keep on the good side of the boss and so they are quite likely to approve of his ideas even when they may not be the best, in the manner of "yes men" and sycophants. They also function to shield him from influences contrary to their designs, and filter and color the information that he does receive.

On the other hand, the president has handy scapegoats when things go really wrong, blaming, for instance, bad input or suggestions from his team. And in this way a poorly functioning system can limp along for years, with a leader well protected from blame or removal.

The critically important aspect, though, is the extra buffering in the organization as briefly described above. Assuming that no meltdown occurs drawing the attention of the international team, the president can use this buffer time to try to learn his role as he goes, having time to switch strategies willy-nilly, minimizing damage from wrong decisions and maximizing any lucky good ones.

The Payoff

The payoff for the boss in this case clearly manifests itself in the form of the retention of a lucrative position, with industry and civic visibility, and having the wherewithal at one's disposal to pursue individual personal goals at one's leisure.

With luck and enough buffer, a poor leader may be able to learn and grow into his responsibilities; without luck or enough buffer, a meltdown and management shakeup may be imminent.

E. D. Everett

I Didn't Do It!

A president or CEO will gladly accept ultimate responsibility when things go wrong. He realizes each failure as a learning opportunity, a chance for continuous improvement in his company's procedures and products. He must demonstrate that he is in charge and capable. He must be an example for his subordinates such that they stand for their individual departments as he stands for the company as a whole.

Not a chance...

The question of who's really responsible is a trick question. The goal, as I have seen, is to have *nobody* in charge! That is to say, there may be a CEO or president who is nominally responsible for the health and well-being of the organization, taking credit and blame in stride, but if he is on his game he can avoid most, if not all, responsibility.

One way to accomplish this goal is to adopt the popular modern "team" approach to management by setting up, for example, an executive council, board of directors, management team or a similar group. The management team will make all of the major decisions of the company. The CEO can populate this group with his VPs and act as the team moderator as they have meetings and discussions, create outlines and forecasts, implement initiatives, etc., in a brave show of due diligence toward company matters. Why, see here, the president has gone to great lengths to assemble a crack team of experts, gather varied opinions, weigh pros and cons, and hash out the best direction for the future. In this way the "team" is responsible for any actions, but *not any one individual*.

The team approach is especially popular in companies where managers are selected from among the workforce and promoted up the ladder. By definition, these "managers" are not, by training, managers; they are knowledgeable in the areas that they were promoted from, be it technical, sales, service or whatever. They may or may not have management skills and the odds are, in my opinion, less than 50-50 that they will. The reason is straightforward: If they had management skills, it is probable that they would have recognized this early in their career and pursued training and employment in that capacity. Of course, companies may offer management training, but a person who has devoted considerable effort in becoming proficient in a non-managerial position may not, at the deepest level, be capable of picking up the skill set required. Without the required skills, managers need a team approach to decision-making because it is likely that they don't know the right thing to do and can't trust their instincts.

Team management offers a further benefit to a weak president; he can solicit opinions and weigh them, taking a sort-of "average" or consensus approach to decisions.

Why This Works

It works because responsibility is diffused across a team. When the team makes a bad decision, policy or statement, the blame falls on no one person; it falls on the management team. Any individual member escapes blame—it was the team's decision, not his. Furthermore, in a grotesque distortion of professionalism, realizing that an error is commonly known amongst the employees, the CEO may actually benefit from increased stature by, later, appearing to stand tall and strong against said flawed decision, policy or statement in front of the workers and pledge to right the wrong. It is an amazing sight to behold. There is something to be said for a management structure that cannot fail to reflect in a positive manner on the CEO.

As good as this system is for the CEO, it's even easier for those managers who are one level under the top to escape responsibility. At this VP level managers have enough power, like the CEO, to populate their subordinate positions with those friendly to their style and objectives, or with those ignorant of the real motives of their boss.

Then, with VP authority and his posse installed, the same benefits and insulation accrue as they do to the CEO and his management team. When things go awry, the VP can transfer blame to his own team or set up one individual as a scapegoat thereby protecting himself as long as possible. When there is no way to escape blame himself, the VP has one additional dimension of protection that the CEO does not; as a last resort he may deflect the blame *upward* to the CEO's team if he is not already a member of that august group, or blame the CEO himself if he is a member— risky behavior that sometimes cannot be avoided.

The Payoff

Escaping blame and responsibility for one's actions, needless to say, is a powerful incentive. Once this trick is learned, it is self-perpetuating.

E. D. Everett

No Such Thing as a Million Dollar Mistake

Management, among other obligations and responsibilities, should tend to the business of keeping the organization running smoothly, always on the lookout for ways to implement continuous improvement, ways to increase productivity, margins, and morale.

Wake up and smell the (expensive) coffee...

Managers, even those at the very top of the ladder in an international company, are only human. And, if, like many I have known, they are managers by promotion rather than by training, they may or may not have the skills to execute their power in a meaningful and helpful manner. Or, if they *are* managers by education and vocation, they cannot, as humans, be expected to be infallible. Sometimes they get sold a bill of goods, just as you or I may.

Imagine if you will a well-dressed, charming visitor in the lobby of the company world headquarters waiting for his appointment with the president or board of directors of your firm. He knows what he is about and shows it. He has already teased the president with enough information to get this appointment, and he regards this opportunity very seriously.

Once admitted, he says all the right things, makes all the right gestures, and convinces the president that he needs to see a full presentation of his, the visitor's, product. Either at this meeting, or a follow-up, the presentation is made. It is a product that promises to improve employee morale, instill corporate values, and promote the company's vision. This is not a fly-by-night operation nor is it a scam; no, it is a fully developed program which reaches from the top levels down, eventually reaching every single employee.

It is not a hit-and-run program either; it is a multi-year affair requiring a major commitment from the company and an all-or-nothing attitude. A short impressive list of big name company references is offered. The visitor thinks it is right for this company and knows that the leaders have the intelligence and foresight to realize what a boon this will be, how they will be respected and, yes, admired for their decision.

And it's a done deal—your company is now the proud purchaser of a "Cultural Edification" program that will be implemented over the next five to 10 years and will involve every single employee working his way through the individual stages. Of course, we must start at the top, including a train-the-trainer approach such that the employees first exposed and indoctrinated into the program can then become the trainers for the next level and so forth from then on.

Our well-dressed salesman is now totaling up his profits, adding one more company to his list of references. He has graciously made himself available for consulting work in the future, at a price, should the momentum of the program flag or if a refresher pep talk is required at any time. However, the success of the program, of course, rests with the company and the resolve of the leaders to push it through.

And push they will, especially the person or persons who made the decision to buy this program. Once a multi-million dollar expenditure is made, there is a very strong tendency for those involved with the purchase to never, ever admit that it could have been an expensive mistake. "Absolutely not, the decision has been made and, by glory, we are going forward" is the general thrust of their response to the idea that an error could have been made.

After a year or so, as all the levels, world-wide, of management had been through stage one of the program, it came down to the employees at our smallish outpost to participate. This turned out to be a two-day affair, including a *mandatory* overnight stay at a local hotel. Obviously, this caused a disruption is our day-to-day work and our group had to go in teams so as not to shut down the operation completely.

Disturbingly, a good deal of the time was spent on getting in touch with our emotions in sessions of amateur psychology. *These sessions were run by managers or hand-picked employees, not by professional educators or trained psychologists.* There were a number of raised eyebrows, but any questions were answered in such a way that it was clear that these sessions would go forward and that participation was mandatory. In my particular group, there were two people who ended up crying (yes, professional adults crying in front of their co-workers) and who had to leave the session for a period of time to recover.

We next had to write a letter to a fictional friend describing our thoughts openly and honestly about the "edification" so far, and then we were *made to read these letters in front of the whole group.* Again, this proved to be troubling to those who were completely honest about their skeptical view of the proceedings and then found they had to share this with their manager.

In another one of our group's sessions, ideas for improvement were brainstormed. Small, three or four person teams were assigned responsibility to implement and monitor these improvements over the coming months. All of our group's improvement ideas from this session, the last of stage one, were shared throughout the company.

After finishing up with, and I am not kidding, small groups creating finger paintings for our office walls, and other small groups composing and performing *a cappella* songs related to the session topics, the "edification" was over for now.

We were told not to discuss what happened in our sessions with those who had not yet attended theirs.

We had a follow up meeting some weeks later, a regular meeting at our office during normal business hours, in which the brainstorm teams discussed progress or lack thereof in the implementation of our group's improvement ideas with management. One employee asked that since everyone's "edification" had the same format, did the managers, at every level, come out of their sessions with tasks to implement new ideas as did we, the lowest level? The answer: "Yes." Great, said the employee, can you please share with us managements' brainstorm ideas? "Why?" was the response.

Detecting some resistance to answer what should have been a simple question, the employee was forced to say the obvious, namely 1) The managers are supposed to be the best and brightest the company has to offer, 2) they have access to a bigger picture or view of the operation and as such would have ideas that could result in far-reaching impact and 3) they have the power to readily implement the ideas that seem the best.

Unfortunately, this sort of logic, while applauded by the questioner's co-workers, had nothing but a negative effect on management. At no time were any of the brainstorming ideas from management's "edification sessions" shared with the general workers. One wonders why.

Moving on, it seems, although it was never communicated as such, that feedback regarding the first stage of the program affected the methods used in the second stage. Most, but not all, of the touchy-feely tasks were removed; leaders from another division, people who none of the workers in our division knew, were used to lead some of the sessions (this I presume was in lieu of getting outside professionals who were trained to handle sometimes emotional atmospheres); finger painting was replaced with creating a group video illustrating some positive change that needed to be implemented; and a group one-act "play" with props was written to present a departmental change idea to a VP.

That there were changes implemented in the second stage brought hope to me and some others that perhaps management was awakening to the fact that this "edification" was a bill of goods that the company directors had bought into and that was being foisted on all the rest of us regardless of the total cost, which included hotels, travel for the non-local participants, time lost from actual work, etc. Instead, it was made perfectly clear that the company plans to forge ahead and complete several more stages of the program during the upcoming years. The fact that this scam gives management something to do and focus on is a plus for them, and must give a certain percentage of them a feeling of accomplishment or at least of direction.

By the way, in neither stage that I attended was there much, if any, mention of what I consider to be our company's primary function: Selling hardware, software and services at a profit. Sadly, there was also little to no mention of legality, ethics or morality.

Why This Works

At the highest levels of management, as at the lower levels, there is a need to "manage" —much as a legislator feels he must participate in adding one more law to the ever-increasing number of laws already on the books whether its addition is justified or not— and to appear as a functioning manager, even when this may not be the case. An easy way to accomplish this is to subscribe to a ready-made program and then oversee the implementation of it, the supposed improvements in the intangibles of morale or company spirit and shared vision more than compensating for the expense.

The Payoff

The person duped into buying the package can then relax, his legacy assured. He may smile and survey all of the activity while receiving numerous reports of the tasks assigned and completed as the implementation trickles down to each and every employee.

E. D. Everett

What Did the President Know and When Did He Know It?

When hiring for middle and upper management positions, especially where management of people is involved, it is always wise to gather as much information as possible about the prospective employee. Traditional references are a must and there is also much to be learned from those who may have had experience with a candidate when in a former position at another company.

Sadly mistaken...

In a specialized industry, where it seems everyone knows everyone, there are plenty of sources of information about a potential management candidate. Current employees and industry contacts will surely have useful information. Of course this information must be carefully weighed and filtered.

If the person doing the hiring is smitten by the glib talk of a candidate, likes his jokes, believes that negative stories about the candidate are simply sour grapes, or for any reason discounts and ignores the available information, he does so at his and the company's peril.

A sad and costly example occurred a few years back when our company president filled an important position with an industry insider with whom many people, including myself, had direct personal experience. In my case, I had worked under his chain of command a few years previously at one of our direct competitors.

Back then, as a newbie in the field service department at this previous company, I got an old beat-up company car that was sitting unused in the parking lot. They called it the vomit comet for a reason. It was to be a temporary measure, and I had been able to put in an order for a new car so that this junker could be retired. It would be a couple months before the new one could be picked up so I made the best of it, cleaning what I could and using air freshener to good effect. The heap also had some wear issues but it didn't make sense to put any money into it for so short a time.

Anyway, at long last, my shiny new burgundy Chevy Lumina was in, and I made arrangements to drop off the old one and make the swap. A very nice feeling it was, now, to be driving something new and safe and clean. I got up early the next morning to take it to the office so I could load up my tools and spare parts before anyone else was in, and I parked right in front of the main doors.

The hero of our story, the then company president, pulled in at the same time, saw the car and made some comment about it, "Looks good!" or something like that. We both went in and I went on my way getting set to take off on the road and get to work. After the receptionist came in, I was paged to come to the lobby with my car keys. I assumed that I needed to move it away from the front doors since we had officially opened for the day, but no. The receptionist said she needed to have my keys because the president liked what he saw and would take the new car for himself. It was back to the vomit comet for me.

The damage done to morale by an incident such as this is significant; the clear sense of the arrogance and pettiness of this person is still with me today.

Imagine my dismay when this same man was hired for an important role at my current company, overseeing a number of technical and sales personnel. I remember vividly the prediction that was made at the time his hiring was announced. "When he leaves, his pockets will be full and that department will be a smoking crater."

That is exactly what happened. After a few years, the complaints, internal and external, were too many ignore and he was unceremoniously let go along with his cronies (whom he had hired after coming on board) amid rumors of near-mutiny by his employees and of a dual set of books for the department—one for the auditors and one real.

Why This Works

It works only when someone in charge believes what he wants to believe, makes decisions based on incorrect assumptions or information, and has the power to act on those assumptions or information.

The question that comes to mind for me is this: Since this man's reputation preceded him, and since there are so many people ready and willing to attest to his low character, how is it that our president came to hire him at all? I see only two possible answers. The first is that the president *didn't know* of this person, nor did he know of his reputation, nor did anyone inform him. This is unlikely in the extreme as they are both long-term players in the industry and in the same geographical area.

The second possible answer is that he *did know* and he's OK with it. Neither possibility reflects well on the president; the company will be paying a long time for this mistake.

The Payoff

I can only guess at what payoff there must have been for the president in this case. Maybe they are personal friends; maybe he was fed a line and swallowed it; maybe the feeling of power that results from giving a lucrative position to someone as a "second chance" overtook common sense. What we do know for sure is that there are many persons qualified for a position such as this without having to scrape the bottom of the barrel to locate them.

Whatever the real reason was, one thing is certain. A plum position was filled with an industry insider and, to those who don't know the reputation and history of this person, the president receives kudos for making a difficult and important decision by hiring an experienced professional.

E. D. Everett

HR Run Amok

A human resources department has a number of important responsibilities. They include the attraction, selection, training, assessment, and rewarding of employees, while also overseeing organizational leadership and culture, and ensuring compliance with employment and labor laws.[3]

Don't make me laugh...

In my experience, HR is complicit in the foibles and follies of executive management and actively works *for* management and *against* the low level employee. At the same time any number of initiatives are in play that are meant to disguise this fact. One common example is the hotline to call when you know or suspect that someone has violated the company code of conduct.

To some, this idea sounds attractive: Help improve the overall standard of business practice by anonymously flagging violations. But, it stands to reason that the higher a person is in an organization, the greater the potential for more damage affecting more persons. And so, it seems more likely that a well-placed person would be turned in than a common Joe. But does anyone who needs his job feel comfortable turning in a superior? If anybody thought this was really an *anonymous* tip number, the lines would be jammed: There had better be operators standing by.

I have observed that this kind of "turn-in-your-co-worker" program is perceived by the general employee as a dangerous sham. It is a good example of HR and management working together.

---

[3] Wikipedia, accessed on August 12, 2013

Why This Works

It works only because HR and executive management form a united front. They each support and protect the other. To successfully breach this wall, one would have to go outside and take legal action, something that is too risky and expensive for most, me included.

Here is another good example. Two job postings came out at roughly the same time. As a long-term employee with experience in several departments, I applied for both positions. One was a promotion within my department to manager; the other would be a move to the sales department as a regional manager for a newly-created region. Problem number one: Both of these applications require the employee's current manager's approval to be submitted. What? I need approval from my boss to apply for a position? For the first position, it doesn't matter as the manager spot is under him anyway. For the sales position, why do I need approval from my current boss to apply for a job outside his department? Suppose he doesn't want me to move to the sales department? Will he deny the application? If so, this is certainly wrong.

Now, after waiting approximately four *months* for a response to either application (that's right, not an official "thank you for applying" letter, email or verbal response) I initiated contact with HR and was told that there is a policy that an employee can apply for only one position at a time. What? When were they going to tell me this? I couldn't find the policy so I asked for a copy or a link to the policy. No response. I kept asking and would not give up until one day I got a call from the HR rep and he told me verbally that he 'made up' the policy. There is no actual policy. Now, that is a stunning admission from the HR rep who is supposed to ensure policies are followed and employees are treated fairly.

When I talked this situation over with my boss (who, by the way, is an officer of the company) he said that he thought the HR rep "made a mistake and didn't know how to get out of it." Somehow an HR rep making up policies and lying about them while stonewalling an employee as long as possible seems more than a "mistake." It seems to me it is gross misconduct and behavior worthy of termination. But wait, there's more!

After the stonewalling and fabrication admission it was announced that the sales position has been filled. Again, no "we are sorry but the position you are seeking has been filled and we will keep your application on file" notification to me either on paper, in an email or verbally. I again contacted HR and asked what happened. Well, at the time of the "two simultaneous applications not allowed" fabrication, someone somewhere decided that I needed to apply for only the position within my department; *I was never considered for the sales position.*

When I questioned the VP of sales about this, he said that he was told (by whom, he wouldn't say) that I really didn't want the sales position and so he never considered me. Someone in management or HR (or both) had decided for me which career path I might be allowed to choose. The end result is that it took approximately six months to learn that one of my applications was entirely disregarded.

(Suspiciously, and relevant to a different aspect of abuse, it slipped out that the sales position was filled by a former coworker of one of our managers when that manager was at another company.)

After that, I asked my boss point blank if the other position, the department manager position, would be filled and would I be considered for it. He answered "yes" to both questions. I waited. After one year with the position being open, still with no response, no interview, no indication of any movement, I formally withdrew my application from consideration.

To be sure, if I had been kept in the loop as to the status of my applications—had I at least been given a shot at interviewing for the positions—the appearance of propriety could have been maintained.

And so, this becomes a good example of a very frustrating and opaque situation wherein management and HR seem to be operating in tandem supporting and protecting each other, with my own boss downplaying the misconduct of HR.

The Payoff

In this case, on the side of the sales department position we can see a multi-faceted lust for power, control and empire-building. If jobs are to be handed out as perks and rewards, then just this sort of manipulation must occur. It can occur between middle managers such that they can determine who gets which jobs and when, and they can strive to keep control of the knowledge and of the back-channel methods used to put this sort of shameful practice into action.

On the other side, the side of the non-sales position, the seemingly endless delay in filling the opening in my department means that the department is running with one headcount short for months (and years—two and counting, at the time of my leaving), with the department employees picking up the slack, thereby saving the department budget a ton of money. It is always a feather in the cap of any manager who can run his department lean.

The payoff, if you're the HR representative, is less clear but probably resides in the security and good will generated by "playing ball" with the powers that be, and through the knowledge that the recipients of your aiding and abetting "owe you one."

At the end of the day, a non-insider (me) was kept out of management, the "old boys club" remained intact, and one manager's empire increased by one.

Neo-Cronyism

Management should proscribe cronyism in any form including nepotism. While in the past such practices may have been common, even expected, the competitive nature of the business environment today forces a business to seek the best employees and business partners, period. Companies cannot afford to hire or do business with someone simply because they are a friend or relative.

Look out for reality...

About a week after we had mandatory company-wide ethics training, an email from HR was sent out informing us that one of our employees, let's call him Matt, was given a new position working directly under Biff, an influential manager of key accounts. Now, this raised a lot of eyebrows amongst us workers for a number of reasons. First, the position was not posted by HR. No one knew there was an opening and no one, to our knowledge, was interviewed for the position. Second, it was a newly-created position and a newly-created title. Third, Matt is a neighbor and friend of the family of his new boss, Biff. Fourth, Matt's brother, Jim, also works for Biff in a similar but different capacity. Fifth, Matt was a relatively new employee with little work experience.

To add insult to injury, a VP, whom many of us work for either directly or otherwise, came through the building the morning of the announcement very chipper and smiling. Not a word did he mention of the promotion. We employees, on the other hand, in a discussion over lunch that day debated if we should call the new ethics violation hot line. But, we said to ourselves, who do you turn in when this move is already approved by HR and upper management? Remember, our own boss seemed pleased and unconcerned this very morning.

One blatant move like this may not seem like much but let's put more context around it. Biff now has multiple neighbors, friends, relatives and former employees all working for the company in various capacities in the same building. And these are only the current *known* connections with direct employees. There have been others in the past and will undoubtedly be more in the future.

I was stunned one day when I walked into a local jewelry store on my lunch hour to price a gift for my wife. I had a company logo shirt on and the salesman who talked to me said, "We see a lot of your people in here!" I asked who and he said, "Biff, Matt, Jim..." and he named most of the gang. "It's a real family affair over there," said he. A random visit, in a random store, with a random salesman —even he knows it's a "family affair." Amazing!

Why This Works

With a weak president and with patience and persistence, a good manipulator can have his way. And some of the moves, maybe all, can be rationalized after a fashion. One department may have high turnover, so it makes some sense to hire someone we already know, right? And they won't be working in the same chain of command, so there is no real conflict, right? And if one of those cronies happens to marry an employee, so what? We are asked to forget that the new spouse was also a friend of the Biff family even before she was hired. It's a little harder to justify the hiring of friends and neighbors, but hey, they don't have the same last name as Biff, so these moves are a little more opaque to the general employee, to international management and to HR.

However it is explained, it is blatant neo-cronyism, as I call it, and is obviously accepted by HR and upper management, apparently unconcerned that someone will stand up, blow the whistle and topple the house of cards.

The Payoff

A company's management team that allows and actively participates in cronyism and nepotism has failed to recognize the danger it presents and the damage it does. Yes, it is easier to find and hire family and friends than to do a proper applicant search, it is pleasurable to give them positions and compensation, keeping it in the family if you will, and it reduces stress if one bends to peer pressure and goes along with this pattern, once it has become entrenched. For certain managers, weak managers, these are the obvious payoffs.

E. D. Everett

Executive Firewall

Executives at the vice president level must have qualities similar to those of the president. Each must show competence in managing the people and performance of his department, take credit and blame where appropriate, and defer to the final authority of the president. Like the president, he must be an example of leadership, professionalism and ethics.

As if!

Unfortunately, the above description does not apply to many of the VPs I have worked with and under. If a company is set up with a number of VPs and if the environment allows, it is likely at least one will be of the type who is working strictly for his own benefit, not the company's.

When the conditions are right, such as when a company has a weak president, easily influenced and fooled, there are those opportunists out there ready and willing to take serious advantage. Even in a company blessed with upper management of good character, it is only a matter of time before the rotten apple finds his way in. Once inside the company, he may have to play along for a time to reach a high level, but when he does, Katie bar the door.

While a VP level position is an important position, it is less so than the CEO's and it has substantially less visibility—both without the organization and within. A person in this position of the right ilk can, in his effort to work toward his personal goals, insulate himself from responsibility, from interaction with others in the company, and to a large extent, completely insulate himself from having to do anything at all unrelated to those goals.

Why This Works

It works because of the structure set up by the executive himself and here is what I have personally seen:

Step one for our manipulative VP is to insert as many of his cronies and those friendly to his way of thinking into his department as possible while at the same time weeding out by transfer or termination the rest. His immediate group of subordinates must be a loyal group of "his boys."

An administrative assistant is a vital next step. The assistant can block many, if not all, persons from physically or electronically contacting the VP. If someone does manage to accidentally get through, one of the subordinate posse is immediately assigned to deal with that person now and into the future. By repeating this action each time there is a breach, in a short few weeks or months all access can be eliminated.

At the same time, it is critical that communication from the president or CEO is *not* blocked and is, in fact, encouraged and solicited. The CEO must be carefully and deliberately supplied with an impression that the VP is doing a good job and is on top of all issues pertinent to his position. This means that the VP must be in nearly constant contact with his boss or at least know where he is at all times, know what he is doing, know where he is going next, and to whom he will be speaking and why.

This configuration, with employees and procedures to block access, means that the VP has a number of ways to avoid responsibility and, further, can avoid any work-related action at all in extreme cases. Should any misstep or error be traceable back to his level, the VP will have a credible case for claiming he never received any communication about the error or incident and therefore knew nothing about it. If this does not work to protect him, he will have already installed at least one expendable subordinate to take the fall for him, keeping his position safe and protection intact.

The Payoff

The perpetrator of these acts of insulation seeks power, protection and autonomy, each in some degree. He enjoys the semi-independence of his position, reaps executive compensation with limited effort (aside from the effort dedicated to setting up his "kingdom"), relaxes in the company of his posse, and works to ensure that these and any other personal goals are obtained and/or perpetuated as long as possible.

E. D. Everett

Inside Job?

A company should always be on the watch for employees showing both an aptitude and desire for promotion. A company, too, should always be on the lookout for employees who are willing and able to take on more responsibility, or those who wish to alter their career path so as to be more in line with their skills and desires. The employee thus recognized should have a background commensurate with the duties and responsibilities required for his potential new position. Lacking this, additional education may be required or provided. Grooming employees such that they become long term assets is beneficial both to the employee and company. When necessary, the company should look outside for competent candidates to fill key positions, but it is a wise business decision to post openings internally first.

Wrong again!

The good positions—those that will prove lucrative, highly visible, or are otherwise plum positions—must be reserved for hand-picked persons and certainly not be wasted on a mere "employee." On the other hand, positions that are not suitable as perks or rewards *should* be posted. These latter are the positions that everyone knows involve hard work and/or low pay and/or long hours. These are "jobs," not perks.

Positions and promotions are perks to hand out to persons a) who will increase the manager's chance of reaching his personal goals; b) who have the same or similar mind-set as the current management team; and c) who will further promote the business-as-usual paradigm and thereby perpetuate existing practices.

As the reader may rightly guess, promotions based on this principle often result in incapable or inept managers. But—and this is key—incapable or inept managers may be an unavoidable but acceptable outcome *if the promotion advances the goals of the promoter.*

It is true that some departments, especially those that are highly technical in nature, cannot function without a competent person in charge. These positions are reserved for those employees deemed promotable but who are not "players," i.e. are not part of the corrupt team.

Why This Works

This unwritten policy only partially works. It is blatantly obvious that something very wrong is happening, but management and HR act as one in obscuring the issue. An after-the-fact email stating "please welcome so-and-so to his new position and wish him luck as he brings a wealth of experience and is uniquely qualified blah blah blah" is sent company-wide; essentially, in its own way, challenging someone to complain. And so we are left to literally take it or leave it—not good for employee morale to say the least.

In the film "Notorious," when one of the lead characters makes a serious blunder that threatens his life and the lives of his associates, one of them says to him, "We are protected by the enormity of your stupidity, for a time." [One of the best lines in all of moviedom, IMHO.] In our context, this means that people will sometimes not immediately recognize a mistake or injustice if it is blatant or *too* obvious. As a person who goes to work every day and tries to do the right thing, I used to assume that others were trying to do the same regardless of their level in the organization. *This assumption is wrong.*

I and others would sometimes discuss questionable promotions that occur and, unbelievable to me now, we would actually make up reasons that "explain" the decision such as "Management must know what they are doing," and "The boss can see the big picture from his level, we cannot. From up there, everything must make sense," or "Tom must have some expertise or background in …" and so forth.

In my recent experience, our team was called into a meeting with our boss, a VP. Without any preliminary discussion he called in and introduced our new boss, to whom we would now report. Mind you, this announcement was without any warning, hint or rumor. Our new boss, let's call him Billy, would now report directly to the VP and be a buffer between the team and the VP.

This announcement was met with a general stunned silence. The newly created position was not posted either internally or externally. It came with a manager title and responsibilities, and included a company car. It was a disconcerting moment since any one of the team was more than qualified for such a new position, and since the new arrangement was, in effect, a demotion of the entire team down one level from the VP. The VP, in the uncomfortable silence, must have felt a need to "explain" the move and said, "Billy is uniquely qualified for the position." We mumbled some well-wishes and the meeting was soon over.

Now, "uniquely qualified" sounds legitimate and, in fact, sounds just like one of the made-up reasons that we would sometimes concoct ourselves over lunch as mentioned above. But it's not. If you think about it *everyone* is uniquely qualified in their own way. Everyone's background and experience is unique; everyone is unique.

Disturbingly, Billy is a neighborhood acquaintance and "adopted son" (not in the legal sense, but in a paternal/protective sense) of one of the key players in the organization. Billy is not the best or brightest the workforce has to offer; I would say he was the *least* qualified for the position of anyone in that meeting, but he has a very influential person in the organization who is shaping his career. In hindsight, it is clear that the position was created simply to make a cushy spot for Billy.

The Payoff

The power of controlling who gets a position, and thereby access to compensation, including commissions and perks, medical benefits, and so forth must to the right person be like an intoxicating drug, as evidenced by the incredible amount of self-delusion required not to see that the ruse is commonly perceived amongst the troops and by the level of arrogance required to persist in this behavior.

In the specific case above, there is an additional dimension of peer pressure amongst managers. One in up to his neck in the "game" would certainly want to abide by the "play along to get along" culture to minimize waves.

Management by Doing Nothing

A good manager will always respond appropriately and in a timely fashion to issues that are brought to his attention.

Not even close...

There are exceptions, but this obvious truth does not hold for many managers. Yes, it is true that a smart manager will respond immediately to all issues brought to his attention *by his superiors*, if he knows how the game is played. But some have learned that no response is the best solution for those requests that come to him from below his level.

It is interesting to walk through the mail room and look at the row of mail slots for in-house employees. The empty slots belong to those employees who come to work expecting to get something done, who are responsible and responsive. For example, I, while certainly not a perfect employee, would check my mail slot at least once a day to make sure there was nothing sitting there that needed my attention.

The slots that are stuffed to overflowing are those of —you guessed it—generally managers. Again, not all are the same, but if you get stuck with a boss who has learned this technique, you will recognize it in short order. The mail slot does not get emptied, emails do not get answered, the requested action or decision does not get taken or made, and phone calls go to voice mail.

It is an annoying situation, especially if there is something that needs to be done that falls outside of your authority to accomplish. Beyond annoying, it can be detrimental to business and your ability to do your job. It falls to the employee to wonder if the situation requires that he re-request the action, possibly irritating the boss, or that he escalate the situation above his boss, again risking the boss' ire.

Why This Works

The answer is simple. It is learned behavior. Let's say you don't mow your lawn for a few weeks. Your neighbors get disgusted and do it for you just to have it done. Voilà, problem solved without you having to lift a finger! Let's see, how long do I have to wait before they will cut the lawn again? Say, the house could use a new coat of paint...

Of course, in a subdivision, the neighbors don't work for you and you can't fire them. At some point they will rebel and call you to task or send a bill. In the corporate environment, it's different. The employees below you may take care of the issue themselves but they will be taking a personal risk should they decide to call you to task.

In my experience, the workers themselves will solve many of the managers' issues simply because the decisions or actions can't be put off any longer. In one case a special device was needed for a particular job that required a large amount of data manipulation and storage. The customer was waiting, and calling the project manager for the results. To wait for the department manager to act on the request to purchase *and* to get him to approve the dollar amount, a doubly difficult assignment, was too much for the employee. Instead, he drove his personal car on his personal time to a local supplier and used his personal funds to get the hardware needed to take care of the customer. I believe his idea was to submit the purchase on an expense report and hope for approval later, after the customer's request was satisfied. In any case the immediate problem was solved, the employee took care of it, and the manager did nothing.

Well, not exactly nothing. One thing that happens is that the workers will eventually recognize this management technique and proactively take care of issues that they can without troubling the manager at all. The manager *has* accomplished something: He has trained his employees not to expect any action or decision and has taught them that they are on their own.

By the way, the manager who knows the right way to handle "doing nothing" will hire an assistant who can make sure the mail slot is empty, screen all emails and calls, and intercept those who may try to contact the manager in person. Nothing changes in the behavior, but at least the mail slot is empty.

The Payoff

Precious time is gained, on the company dime, for an expert in this technique to devote to pursuing his personal goals. Once they realize the futility of the situation, the constant barrage of questions and requests from one's employees dries up, and so does the annoyance of having to deal with them. As long as the work of the department gets done and the bosses above are happy, this is a management strategy for personal success that works!

E. D. Everett

Si Señor

The company should periodically review and reward employees based on merit—how well they perform their assigned functions, how well they fit into the company's structure, and their level of integrity and professionalism.

Remove head from sand...

It is anathema to a company to base raises on merit. This can lead to lawsuits and other unpleasantness if it appears to be favoritism in someone's eyes. The merit raise should be eschewed in favor of the seniority raise, the small, across-the-board raise given to all active employees. If at all possible, however, an employee should be made to *feel* as if he has been given a raise based on merit when in reality every employee who is breathing at the time gets the same boost in pay. The slackers, the disgruntled, even the ones actively working *against* the best interests of the company get the same raise as the best and brightest.

Why This Works

It works if management can keep those workers who would prefer to be recognized for exemplary performance from finding out about this practice, or by treating on a case-by-case basis those who do recognize the deceit and decide to protest.

Believe it or not, I have had my manager, a VP, call me into his office, close the door, and tell me of a raise that I would be receiving. He made it seem as if it were just for me, and that it was based on my efforts on the job, and as such indicated not to discuss it outside of his office. Of course, I was flattered and pleased with myself, vowing to redouble my dedication to the company's business. However, lo and behold, one of my co-workers in another department let it be known that he also received a raise of the same amount as mine effective at the same time! Others chimed in as well until it became apparent what had been done. It was an across-the-board seniority raise; it didn't matter one whit about performance or if one was an above average or below average worker.

If a valued employee calls management on this practice or in some way demands to be considered for a raise commensurate with his talents, the employer may respond by making a change in the plaintiff's title such as adding the prefix "Senior" or suffix "Specialist." In some cases, a brand new title will be created and the "new position" comes with a salary hike equivalent to a raise.

The creation of new titles to compensate employees can be taken to extremes. One service department worker, by blowing the whistle on certain middle managers whom he caught ethically misbehaving, received as his reward a new position, title and compensation as "Select Advisor to the President." Perhaps uncomfortable with the way he was promoted, he never took a desk in a cubicle, of which there were several open, but *stood* at a small table in the hallway where he did his "work" on his laptop. For *three years* he did this until being re-assigned to another area. Tellingly, the position of "Select Advisor to the President" has never been re-filled and I have often asked, "Who is performing the critical functions that this employee did for those three years? Hmm?"

The Payoff

Why conduct proper employee reviews? Why waste the time and effort to evaluate each employee on actual performance and output when it is simpler and less risky to give out across-the-board raises? It certainly doesn't require any special effort on the part of a manager, easing the burden of having to monitor what is happening in his department and who is doing it.

It seems to me that exceptionalism and excellence are slowly being weeded out of the workplace in favor of employees who are willing to go along to get along, as the saying goes. See no evil, hear no evil, speak no evil—just do your job and be happy with your 2%

raise and pay no attention to the fact that the cost of living has gone up 4% in the same year.

E. D. Everett

Last Man Standing

In making decisions, a manager should look at the facts, assess the options, discuss the situation, if necessary, with trusted advisors and industry experts and then render a timely decision that he can justify, stand behind and enforce.

The answer is blowin' in the wind...

In the case of weak management a different approach may soon become apparent. If a manager does not relish the task before him, is not up to the task, or simply is readily influenced by others, he may choose to opt for the easy way out: Take from someone else the idea which sounds best at the moment and go with it. Or, as in my experience, a certain manager would not just listen to others for the *best* idea but he would adopt the *last* idea he heard before the decision deadline. In other words, the last person in front of him before the decision has to be made, if he has a reasonable-sounding idea, has a good chance of seeing that idea taken and used.

Now, this is not necessarily a bad thing. With competent advisors, it really may be the exact right thing to do. However, once this style is known amongst his employees a light will go off in at least some of their heads. If they want to influence the direction of decisions such that they enhance their personal goals, they simply need to be in the right place at the right time. And the more aggressive they are, the more they can make sure they "happen" to be right there.

I was asked once to provide input for a decision to this manager. I gathered all the relevant data at my disposal and put together what I thought was a cogent argument for a particular decision. In the boss's office during our closed-door discussion of this argument, which was very well received by the way, a certain other employee found it necessary to knock and open the door to issue some comment or question. After we finished and as I was leaving, there was that same interrupter standing right outside the door waiting to enter the instant I left. Lo and behold, the decision went a different way—the way of the interrupter.

I realized later that the interruption was a ruse to see what was going on with the boss and to give an excuse to be the last man in before the decision. After recognizing this, I made a point to see what happens in subsequent meetings with this manager and sure enough our "last man" would nearly always sniff out the fact that someone was talking to, possibly influencing, "his" boss and make some excuse to crash the meeting with an inane comment or question. It got so bad that I used to time how long it would take before he would make an appearance into our conversations. Sure enough, like clockwork he would stick his head in the door.

For me, once I realized the mode of operation of this personality type, I simply resigned myself to it as an irritating reality and learned to laugh at the transparent antics. If the door to the meeting was open, the interrupter would hang out in the line of sight of the boss and try to silently attract his attention. If the door was closed, there would be the knock and a head stuck into the office, without waiting for an invitation to enter mind you, followed by a comment or question that could easily wait until later.

What I don't understand fully is why any boss would allow this behavior to repeat endlessly. Surely he can see through the ruse? Surely knows he's being used? Maybe not.

Why This Works

In this case our manager gets to make a decision without all the pesky work of trying to make the *right* decision. And, if it all goes south, if the decision after all was the wrong one, he has a handy scapegoat to blame.

The Payoff

The payoff for management is as stated above—easy and quick decisions with a handy person to blame for errors. The payoff for the advisor? Influence of company decisions resulting in increased stature in the eyes of the boss, or perhaps a more lucrative situation for himself. As always, the payoff will be to enhance one's personal goals, be they prestige, influence, money or other.

E. D. Everett

Power? Absolutely!

*The power granted to executives must be used wisely. In making
business decisions, hiring and firing, and in their professional
conduct in general, our best and brightest must do their very best for
the company and thereby, in turn, for themselves and all the
employees.*

Have I got a Florida land deal for you!

An executive working the system is working primarily for his
own benefit. He is using all the techniques he can to secure and
expand his "empire." Sometimes, drunk with power, he may go a bit
overboard to say the least.

For example, we had a high-level executive who, after a few
years of positioning and reconnoitering, decided he was safe and
secure enough that he could begin making some additional personnel
adjustments. Just before a holiday break one year, he let two
employees go at the same time. I personally knew both of these
people and had high regard for each of them and for different
reasons. They were knowledgeable, quality professionals, but
nevertheless were let go. Two new hires replaced them and were
trained and in place for a few months when, oddly, one of these was
let go. Again, the one let go was a bright and professional individual.

The remaining new hire was this exec's personal assistant. My
office overlooked the employee entrance and parking lot and,
because of some comments I'd heard, I began to take notice of their
occasional departure, disappearance and return after an hour or two.
Of course this means nothing by itself, business meetings in and out
of the office are standard procedure. But, as the near-simultaneous
departures and returns continued, the taking of two vehicles at
different times faded and they would simply ride together. Later, the

assistant became a traveling companion for this executive, including at least one international trip.

Again, none of this means that anything unseemly was going on. The time spent together on company time could be work related and it certainly must be assumed that this was the case. But the appearance of blatant impropriety was inescapable. Did I mention that each of these parties is married, not to each other, and each with children? It sure seemed like, even if there was nothing untoward going on, that the executive relished the macho image that he was creating and did nothing to quell the suspicion. No, quite the opposite.

After some additional months of this arrangement it became known that these two, the exec and his assistant, had known each other before she was hired. It seems obvious now that the earlier firings, which included the previous assistant, were engineered simply to make room for his friend. And, by the way, she was given quite a lot of power herself and had no problem carrying a grudge and seeking revenge on employees with whom she had run-ins, a very bad situation indeed.

Why This Works

We must assume that for a person who would engage in this type of behavior, short-term gratification outweighs long-term career consequences. For him, it most certainly works for at least some period of time.

But, it only works to the extent it is allowed to work by, in this example, the company president who was the direct supervisor of the executive in question. The president brought shame onto the company and tarnished its image by allowing the firing of good employees to make room for the friend and by letting her be empowered to the extent she was.

The Payoff

The payoff for the executive, presumably, is the kick he gets out of having his friend around almost all the time and having the company pay her to be there, and pay her to do his bidding, and pay her to travel on company trips.

Thankfully, in the long run both the exec and the assistant were unceremoniously let go. The executive was removed first followed by the assistant, who was reportedly last heard screaming to the HR rep "You can't fire me!"

E. D. Everett

Schmoozing

Businesses should be run professionally. They need defined roles and responsibilities for every employee. An organizational chart should be kept updated and published so a clear "line of command" is known and visible to all. The days of secret deals in smoke-filled back rooms are over. No longer will a decision end with a wink and a nod, a slap on the back, and a toast to the privileged party.

Wrong, wrong, and so wrong!

Pay attention to this one because it could start or enhance your career dramatically. Failure to heed it could cost you your position or job.

First, the back room deals as briefly described above cannot happen now as smoking has been almost completely eliminated from the workplace. Seriously though, if any of you out there believes that the "old boys club" is gone, you are mistaken. The "old boys" have been replaced by their modern equivalents and in the right environment a smooth operator can warp and bend a business operation to advance his designs.

To schmooze: to chat in a friendly and persuasive manner especially so as to gain favor, business, or connections.[4] Yes, exactly so. Ladies and gentlemen, if you have this talent, then you can succeed in business without having any other skills at all. Period. To succeed you need to know what you want, be able to recognize someone who can give it to you, and confirm that you can influence that person's decisions. By this last I mean the schmoozer has to have the ability to recognize who he can influence and who he cannot. Once the target has been identified, the schmoozer simply

---

[4] Merriam-Webster.com, accessed on July 19th, 2013

learns the right "buttons" to push and he is off to the races, as it were.

Why This Works

In a company with a weak management structure, managers will, for at least a portion of their careers, flounder as they make decisions. They may choose to seek help and surround themselves with trusted advisors as they try to grow into their positions.

These managers are targets for the schmoozer. The higher he can work into an organization, the better. Not that the schmoozer himself is interested in a promotion per se; he's not. If he can achieve his personal goals working in the shipping department, so be it. But the higher his targets are the better.

How does he do it? I am no schmoozer, but I have seen a bona fide expert, along with a few others of moderate skill, in action over the years and it is an amazing sight to behold. Do you like golf? Cars? Alcohol? Sailing? Whatever it is, once he's got you pegged, it turns out that he has connections at your favorite golf course, and knows the golf pro personally. Or he has a guy down the street who works for peanuts on certain sports cars—just like the model you have. Or he just had dinner with the owner of an upscale wine bar and can hook you up. Or he's booked a sailing trip in the Caribbean, and the other couple has bailed out if you would like to go. Or.... I think you get the picture. Say, he knows someone that could fill that position in marketing that hasn't been posted yet...

If you are the victim of a schmoozer, you may not know it because he will take care to keep you happy and as insulated as possible. It will be his job to know where you are at all times, what you are doing there, and, if possible, what you are thinking. He will also be looking to go over your head and schmooze your boss, so good luck with that. But once he's got you under his influence, the decisions that he will help guide you through will be aimed at achieving *his* personal goals. In my case, I saw the master schmoozer is not primarily interested in compensation, although, don't get me wrong, he was and is making good money—his main thrust is to get and keep family and friends employed. And he does!

The Payoff

The payoffs for successful schmoozing are as varied as the number of goals that one has set for himself. A professional schmoozer can, all at the same time, fill a lucrative position, build an empire, and pull the strings of control for those around him, at, below and above his level.

It's important to note that the schmoozer is operating above board much of the time. In other words, the effects of his manipulations are obvious and open for all to see. He is using the talent that he has to succeed and he's not hiding anything. If I had the same talent and had to rely on it for my career, maybe I would. It is, though, a completely foreign approach to my way of thinking.

No, I fault the rest of the management team for not putting the brakes on his actions. When the schmoozer's actions become a detriment to morale, when good people are overlooked or let go (yes, this can happen) to make room for another crony, neighbor or relative, the schmoozer's exercise of his talent has gone beyond the excusable to become a negative force in the organization as a whole. From the president on down, someone has to stand up and say enough is enough.

E. D. Everett

Dress for Success

A manager should be professional in appearance and behavior. He must represent the company in an ethical manner. He must have the best interests of the company, its customers and its employees at heart.

Um... I don't think so. ...

Many players who are best able to work the system for their own personal gain have the following qualities: they look good in a suit; they *appear* professional; they *seem* ethical; they have a genial manner which *suggests* they can be trusted. They give an *impression* that they are genuinely concerned about doing the right thing, but in truth their aim never varies from the target(s) they have set for their personal goals, whatever those goals may be. All else is obstacle or distraction.

Why This Works

For some, appearance is everything and for them our dapper player can do no wrong. If he can find an influential person who falls for the image and hires him, he is on his way; the bad apple is in the bushel basket. For others, the disconnect between the appearance and the actual becomes more or less quickly apparent. But, if our man has done his job, he can insulate himself effectively from those he can no longer fool and from their criticism.

As long as he can keep a squeaky clean image in the eyes of upper management and limit any damaging communication, he can work this scam indefinitely. I mean, who are you going to believe, a low level peon or a well-dressed, highly-placed, genial executive?

It is thankfully true that when the stench reaches a point where even upper management must take notice and do something, when the rock is finally overturned exposing the disgusting mass beneath, this type of manager usually disappears overnight with, typically, a brief email saying he "has left the company" and we "thank him for all his contributions" and "wish him well in his future endeavors."

The Payoff

A person's good grooming and attention to attire are rewarded by initial respect. First impressions are important, as they say, and as long as the impression lasts long enough to infiltrate a company and begin looting, as long as the appearance leaves a shadow of a doubt when the true personality and intentions begin to show, the payoffs outweigh the short-term nature of this deception.

It must be that a person such as described above recognizes the magic of good looks early in life. Some may not let it influence their personality, but others seem to milk it for all it's worth.

In an image-conscious society such as ours, a Dapper Dan may choose politics or possibly even the field of entertainment for a career. If he chooses industry and has marketable skills, so be it. But woe to his coworkers if he succeeds on good looks alone because they will have to pick up the slack.

If this fellow happens to hook up with a manager of the type we have encountered many times and describe in this book, it is a bad situation. The snappy dresser will do his best to continue to fool his boss and the company, while the manager may in turn use the employee to increase his empire and influence.

As one could guess, as long as the personal goals of both parties are being achieved this relationship has legs and may enjoy a degree of permanence that will strain the credulity of those who see through the ruse.

It is only when the lack of ability or skills becomes so detrimental that it cannot be ignored, cannot be overcome by a warm smile or a new tie, that something must be done.

E. D. Everett

Golden Shield Program

In an ongoing effort to maintain a professional environment, management must constantly be alert to malfeasance, incompetence and any misconduct that may reflect poorly on the organization. By persistently rooting out these evils, the overall integrity and reputation of the company increases. Malfeasance, once identified, will be treated immediately and harshly, incompetence will be dealt with through re-training, transfer, or demotion and misconduct punished according to the severity of the offense.

Life is but a dream...

The naive fail to take into account those persons who are protected. Some employees, through cronyism, nepotism, or other special relationships, can do no wrong. They can fail miserably at their jobs and, although the failure is common knowledge among some of their coworkers, be rewarded through transfer, promotion or simply by being kept on the payroll. Others can embarrass the company on their personal time, and be rewarded by having no disciplinary action taken against them. In fact, it almost appears in some cases that to flaunt their protected status, some employees wear misconduct as a badge of honor.

Several examples of reward in spite of failure at job performance come to mind but one incident of misrepresenting the company while on personal time seems to me to be most egregious and stands out in my memory.

At one of the annual trade shows that we regularly attend, several of the booth staff went out to dinner after the show closed. Our group ate and talked, reviewing the success or failure of the various exhibits in our booth. Eventually, most of us made our way to our respective rooms to rest for the next day of the show. The next morning the following was reported:

A certain small group of up and coming young members of our anointed "in" crowd, all with "manager" in their titles, stayed in the hotel restaurant until closing time. Afterward, in a quest to obtain more alcohol, they turned their attention to the hotel convenience store—the little pantry usually found near the lobby and reception desk—where, during normal hours guests can purchase sundries including beer. Finding this, too, closed, they approached the desk receptionist with the intent, evidently, of convincing her to assist them in their quest. She quite rightly refused. Case closed? No way. At least one of our heroes, we understand, decided to attempt to get the pantry key.

Now some see this behavior as alcohol-fueled boys-will-be-boys humorous prankishness, but others see it as scary and dangerous. The receptionist called security at which point the perpetrators quickly retired to their respective rooms.

So, where are these miscreants working now? No, not at a fast-food restaurant. They are as happily employed as they were before this incident. No visible repercussions were seen and none were announced. In fact one can detect an attitude of invincibility in their demeanor. One can imagine an invisible golden shield which, put in place by their benefactor(s), keeps them from receiving their just punishment.

Although, as far as we know, no charges were filed, it remains to be answered what management's response would be if a non-protected individual was involved in a mess like this.

The details of the incident are not as important, in my mind, as are the markedly different responses of the hotel versus our company's upper management. The hotel banned our company from their facility, at least for a time and we know these events are lucrative for the hospitality industry around exposition sites. The hotel is deliberately turning away a potentially significant amount of cash by taking this stand. In stark contrast, those with the golden shield appear, as unbelievable as it may seem, to benefit from increased stature after the event.

Why This Works

This can only work through the collusion of several departments and managers. One would imagine that their immediate supervisors, upper management, marketing (where the shows are organized and hotels booked), HR and legal would all be involved and complicit in greater or lesser degrees. When this is the case, the misconduct extends beyond the two troublemakers and includes everyone who covers up or ignores their behavior or stands in the way of their punishment.

The Payoff

By keeping the "in" crowd protected, a measure of security is provided to all of those on the "inside." If one of them is caught in a misdeed, the others rally around because, who knows, they may be next in need of protection.

E. D. Everett

The Golden Boot

Sometimes it becomes apparent that an employee is not a good fit for an organization. If re-training, re-assignment and encouragement do not work, it is best to let that person go to find a position better suited to them such that both they and the company can move on and prosper.

Gimme money – that's what I want!

Some people have their aims fixed on climbing up the ladder no matter what. They could care less about right or wrong, despise most if not all people as inferior to themselves, and assume that others are to be used in their quest for money and power.

At one place where I worked many years, we had an employee who, soon after starting with the company, became a middle manager and remained so for most of the 15 years or so he was employed by the organization. He held a number of positions, mostly within the sales department, with a company car, salary, commission and expense account.

He confided in me more than once his desire to eventually be a VP if not president while at the same time he was running down the decisions and "poor judgment" of others and the incumbents.

Unfortunately for him, his aptitude for sales and management was low. At one time he had employees working under him; the stories of his abuse of his power for power's sake would fill a separate volume. Suffice it to say that by the end of his career at this company, he had no one under him. He moved through several departments, but never above middle management. The talk among the other long term employees watching his career was filled with questions about his being retained by the company at all. What is his hold over upper management? What is his expertise?

His last position was in sales and he was tasked to drum up business in a market where we had some penetration, but the potential remained huge. Our international operation had success in this niche but for some reason stateside we were behind their percentage of market share. Anyway, it was his task to get to these potential customers and give this business segment a boost.

After more than a year he, to my knowledge, brought in exactly zero new business and, worse yet, brought in exactly zero of his potential customers for demonstrations. And finally, at long last, he was let go.

End of story? Not at all. I ran into this character a year or so later at one of the industry trade shows. He was gainfully employed by a well-respected company in a different but related segment of our industry. He said he had this new job all lined up for quite some time and was just waiting to get fired from our outfit so he did not have to quit. This way, by getting fired, he would receive a severance package of several months' pay and also be ready to step immediately into his new position. In fact he bragged about working the system while employed with us, collecting his cash, not doing his job, setting up the new job, collecting the severance and moving on when finally we could stand him no more.

Why This Works

Here we have a case where a person who looks normal, dresses well, is glib and never at a loss for words, and possesses an excess of self-confidence can hoodwink upper management for years. He is the equivalent of a sociopath, but executes his amoral behavior in the business environment instead of in society at large. How management lets themselves be used like this can only be explained, in my mind, by their being easily manipulated and fooled into thinking our amoral user is a man of at least *some* substance.

The Payoff

While the victim company loses big time, the business sociopath is handsomely rewarded. He is coddled and groomed, he is handled with kid gloves and moved around trying to find the "right place" for him in the organization, he is given power and compensation—although not enough to satisfy his over-sized desires—and he is given every benefit of the doubt until it becomes painfully obvious to all, even upper management, that he has to go. No matter to him; he's all set up in a new environment and gloating over pulling the wool over the eyes of the last bunch of idiots.

E. D. Everett

Leaning Tower of Managers

It is to the advantage of any business to operate in an efficient manner. Personnel numbers should be streamlined to a point where daily work gets done and there is sufficient coverage to absorb temporary increases in workload. Common sense indicates that vacations, sick time, jury duty and the like must be accounted for in the calculation of the required number of workers. Similarly, the management structure itself must just suffice to handle the optimum number of employees, especially so since managers generally are compensated at a higher level.

If only...

Let's look closer now at the number of managers relative to the number of non-management employees or, as I like to say, workers.

In a company such as ours, the combined "average" company of my experience, there is a strong tendency to promote from within. How this becomes the routine is covered in another section, but it does happen. For example, our last president started as an entry-level employee and was promoted over the years to the top. Similarly, long-term employees, in order to realize some sort of career advancement, pay increase, or simply as a reward for their seniority, generally move up to a position of management over people or product or both; many of our president's early co-workers are still with the company scattered at various management levels.

"Once a manager, always a manager" is a saying because demotion is rare. (It does happen but I have seen more often than not if a manager proves to be incompetent, corrupt or otherwise unacceptable, he is moved laterally into a position when he may be better able to cope or at least do less damage.) At the same time, it is expensive and time-consuming to go outside the company to find, hire and train a replacement for a promoted person. And one cannot be sure if a new hire will work out, or if he will decide to stay for the long run. And so, promoting from within is economically advantageous.

To support this more-or-less constant upward flow of managers, the company must grow in size. And since managers of people generally manage a team or department, company growth has to be significant. At some point, at least as I have seen, the growth in the number of managers exceeds a common sense number relative to the number of underlings.

There is another factor in play. Taking into account the new compensation and perk package for a promoted manager, it behooves upper management to spread the existing workload amongst the remaining peons as long as possible, thereby driving the ratio even higher, at least for a time. It's a double-bonus if the new manager will foolishly assume his new responsibilities while continuing with all or at least part of his former duties.

Slowly but surely the organization becomes top heavy. In the company I am most familiar with, it became very top heavy indeed. Even a simple request for an org chart was reprimanded because, you see, an org chart would expose in black and white the super-abundance of managers and show how few people are doing the actual work of the company. Some departments had one manager and two workers; one department had one manager and one worker. It became a joke among the employees. We decided that the ideal ratio must be to have a manager for every single worker in the company. But then, we realized, what with manager meetings, vacation, business trips, golf, and the like, the ratio should be even higher so that there is no chance that an employee will not have a manager nearby—maybe something like one and one-half managers per worker would do the trick.

Why This Works

The conscientious worker will be primarily concerned about coming to work each day, doing his job the best he can, and trying to stay on the good side of his supervisor; he will not primarily be concerned with counting heads and calculating ratios unless something clearly is awry. If the paychecks keep coming, and overtime is not excessive, there is a tendency to simply do your work and leave all the intrigue to others.

Second, the traditional worker will be somewhat intimidated by his supervisor and other managers because he needs the income and does not want to become "the complainer."

Third, with the apparently endless number of positions for managers with perks, it is always possible that if a worker holds out and keeps his nose clean, there will be a reward for him as well.

Last, the managers themselves certainly know a good thing when they see it. They will strive to grease any squeaky wheels in their department in order to keep their own positions secure.

The Payoff

Here we have a complex of interacting rewards for this behavior. The pleasure of being able to hand out jobs, the comfort of surrounding oneself with buddies and pals with whom one has worked over the years, the protection of having coworkers who are beholden to you for their position—and perhaps more.

It must be noted however that no company can survive if everyone eventually gets promoted to a supervisory position. This may be why it is common to hear complaints from low level managers about the high workload versus lower compensation than expected. *Somebody* has to keep doing the work of the company!

E. D. Everett

Millionaire Salesmen

It is in the best interests of the company to reward the sales team with an aggressive commission incentive structure. The reward percentages and goals will be in line with company goals for specific products but will in no way limit the potential income of the salesman. In this way if a salesman excels and exceeds his targets both he and the company benefit through a higher level of bookings and revenue than would otherwise be obtained.

No way, Jose!

This structure cannot be allowed. First, it would be unseemly to a management team to have lowly salesmen out-earning them. Second, to some in management it is incorrectly perceived as a *disincentive* to the sales team as a whole to have one or two super-star salesmen who outshine the rest.

It becomes a yearly ritual for management to adjust each salesman's commission rate, goals and bonus structure such that 1) he, the salesman, will likely *just miss* his goal or, if lucky, will just barely exceed it and 2) the salesman's total income can be controlled to what the manager or management team *thinks he should be making* in his position.

If the salesman just misses his target, as planned, then the stage has been set nicely for next year's commission discussions such that the manager can counter any argument that the sales guy should get a better deal by saying, "But you didn't reach your goals last year."

By using this method to control total compensation, management can adjust each salesman's contract to the perceived "correct" level each year. Although it's common to hear touted that "there is no upper limit to a salesman's potential income," the reality is quite different. If one member of the team has a home-run year, it can be "corrected" next year by management giving him an impossible goal.

Once, when working in commissioned sales with a yearly contract, I had a frustrating experience with just this sort of manipulation, plus a twist.

My sales goal was set at a high but reasonable level based primarily on previous years' numbers. It was a struggle, but with the help of a large order I made the target, just barely. The large order was for a complex project with an overseas final installation and required multiple quotations, meetings and discussions. Importantly, the value of this one order was about 20% of my entire yearly goal. The final installation site happened to be in the country in which our international headquarters is located although the purchasing agent and technical decision-makers were located here in the U.S.

Well, after several rounds of technical and financial review, my customer did end up placing the order with us. It was a lot of work but certainly worth it in the end, since, as I said, it pushed me just over my goal.

But here's where the twist comes in. At the last moment, after final review and acceptance of our quotation, someone high up in management, probably at our international headquarters, decided that since the product would end up there, and since they had the ability to manufacture the product just as well as we did here in the states, that *they would take the order*.

What this means is that the revenue from the order would show up on their books, not ours. And that, since the customer is also a large international firm, the sales representative that handles them in the final installation country would receive the credit for the order!

When it came time to sit down with my boss, the VP of sales, to discuss next year's contract, I commented that it was a disappointment not to see a raise or other incentive to keep up the good work. His response: "You didn't meet your goal."

Talk about a slap-in-the-face disincentive. I wonder if my sales counterpart at international headquarters got a bonus for exceeding his goal? It's just this sort of shenanigan that makes one question what all the work was for and is one of the reasons that I did not regret my eventual departure from sales.

Why This Works

As you may guess, this doesn't work in the long run for many in the sales profession. The really good salesmen catch on right away. If they don't have the connections or ability to schmooze their way into being a part of the "in" crowd, they leave for greener pastures as soon as possible. Others simply put up with the system thinking that it is the norm (and perhaps they have had similar experiences at another company).

Then there are those who think, dammit, I am going to beat them at their own game and meet my "impossible" goals anyway. These are the ones that management looks for. These are the ones who keep the bookings coming, ones who strive to and do meet impossible goals, all while working for less than they could be earning under a different scheme.

The Payoff

Let's just say it—power and money. Since the manager of a commissioned sales force generally gets a cut of his team's bookings, the less he has to pay out in commission means that there is more left in the pot. If his (the manager's) take were to then be increased a bit, it is less noticeable in the bottom line than if his team were compensated in a more equitable fashion.

And we have already mentioned the power this gives management over his team. He can reward and punish as he sees fit, teaching those who may out-earn him a lesson.

E. D. Everett

Plus vs. Minus

A manager should pay attention to those employees who go the extra mile, put in extra effort, and show that they are concerned about doing more than is minimally required. He should reward those employees when appropriate and, similarly, allow them the benefit of the doubt when their effort seems below par.

O ye fools...

In the mind of a conscientious employee there is a concept of pluses and minuses. "The boss will surely take note when I come in early, stay late, and work above and beyond the call of duty. I know he will then cut me some slack when I need to do a personal errand on company time or if I need to extend my lunch hour a bit."

My experience tells me there is only a concept of minuses in the mind of management. Working nights, weekends, holidays or when sick is expected or at least ignored, while coming back late from lunch one day is regarded with an evil eye and results in a black mark on the boss's mental slate under your name.

One example sticks out in my mind. I worked in my last position before retirement for many years. For the first five years I did not take a single sick day while during that same time put in a lot of OT (this was a salaried position; OT is not paid) to learn the software and perfect the techniques used for my job. During school days for a few of those years, I would drop my son at his school and rather than go home or stop for breakfast would go to the office an hour early. I would sometimes spend weekend days at the office with my kids and work while they would color, watch videos or otherwise occupy themselves. Unlike many employees, my work cell phone remained on 24 hours every day and I took calls whenever they came—weekends, holidays, whatever.

Shockingly, during a review near the end of that first five years, I was scored low on one category only: attendance! I will never forget this insult and the serious discussions with my manager and his supervisor that followed.

Why This Works

It only works in the very short run. Management benefits from this type of behavior because, if the employee doesn't catch on, productivity gets a free boost while the employer monitors and records negatives that may be used in controlling the employee's compensation. The employee, on the other hand, does not benefit from this behavior other than by having the satisfaction of doing a good job and by giving 110%.

This short-sighted behavior does, however, teach important lessons:

- It teaches the employee that no one is tallying extra effort and that he himself is the only one who knows or cares how much time is expended for the company's benefit.

- It teaches that the employee review process is a sham and that a manager must have something to point to, true or not, as an area of improvement such that the raise or reward, if any, for an employee's performance can be controlled.

- It teaches management that they have a fool in their employ who will work long hours and put in extra effort at the same rate of compensation as others who don't.

And, most devastatingly, it has a doubly negative effect on the employee in question. He sees he is being used and tends to pull back on effort without reward. Secondly, he sees other employees, using up all their sick days every year, turning off their phones at 5 pm, arriving late and leaving early, who remain in good graces with management and get compensated the same or better than he. It's a perfect system for stifling productivity, encouraging waste and creating morale problems.

Suffice it to say I learned to cut back on my hours but could never bring myself to shut off the phone or take all my sick time each year.

The Payoff

Aside from using the conscientious employee unfairly to boost productivity, the main reward for this technique is that it replaces true management with a simpler pattern. The manager does not have to think about the nuances of his employees' performance; he treats them all as an overseer would with a virtual whip ready for the slackers.

E. D. Everett

Duplicity

Company goals and policies should be clearly stated. Management should scrupulously abide by current policies both as a matter of good business practice as well as to provide an example for the rest of the employees.

Au contraire, *mon ami*...

Management can and will do whatever the hell it wants any time it wants even if it means blatant contradiction of policy or sudden reversal of direction. This behavior is not to be confused with reasonable mid-course correction when a policy or procedure is clearly broken or wrong-headed. In the spirit of continuous improvement, this latter version of corrective action is to be encouraged and applauded. No, the kind of mismanagement I'm speaking of here is a deliberate violation of policy for the *wrong* reasons.

A mild, but telling example: We had an all-employee meeting in which management solicited ideas to improve business and bring more potential customers into the sales funnel, as it is called. "No idea is a bad idea" was the lead-off statement by the company president and he began the meeting by setting up an easel with markers for recording the ideas generated. There had been no warning for the meeting and thus there was a slow start to the creative process. At last, though, ideas from the assembled workers began to emerge. There was some embarrassment on the part of the volunteers when several of these ideas were discussed and rejected as "already tried that" or "won't work because..." It turns out that some ideas *are* bad ideas after all.

When input dried up (after all, no one wants their idea shot full of holes in front of the whole company) a department manager tried to get things started up again (oddly, the highest paid people in the group were not pressed for ideas, just the peons) by suggesting that an idea would be "to do demonstrations for non-customers." Now, while the demonstration crew puzzled over this confusing statement, the president wrote this gem down as a winner! It was with some measure of satisfaction that, sometime later during a review of the ideas gathered at the meeting, the president asked me what that statement meant, as we typically only give demonstrations to *potential* customers i.e. non-customers, in hopes that they will *become* customers.

Here is a more serious example, one with ethical ramifications. We received a new directive from our president himself that all projects (non-standard products requiring engineering and/or programming, many times using business partners) going out to third parties for quote had to have at least two, preferably more, bids to help control costs for our end customers. By the way, this new policy was to prevent the previously existing common practice of handing jobs to buddies and pals on a whimsical or at least non-professional pretext. Anyway, time went on and up came the very next complex project to be quoted. We had a tactical meeting amongst sales and technical personnel to put together a bid package when, who should open the door but that self-same president. He did not sit down, he did not join the discussion, but simply said, "This job goes to ABC[5] company," his pals with whom he has had a long professional and personal relationship. And he left and shut the door. So much for policy and competitive bidding.

Why This Works

It works only as long as no one puts his job on the line and stands up to the policy violator. If the whistle blower is eliminated, then it works only if no one else will back him up, and so on down the line.

Of course when the president makes a flat statement like that it becomes a question for the team: Do we comply? Do we confront?

---

[5] Not their real name

Do we report (and if so, to whom)? For a president to put his employees in this position is regrettable and unfair, at best.

The Payoff

It's hard to say what goes through the mind of a duplicitous person, especially one, like in the examples above, who has power in an organization. It must be that he follows the path of least resistance, bowing first to a coworker who he feels must be shown respect, and second to the needs or requests of his friends regardless of the best interests of our customers.

E. D. Everett

There *is* a Free Lunch After All

Management should provide proper training for employees when appropriate for their job function. In a multi-shift environment, a key person should be assigned who, once trained and familiar with the department's requirements, can be the in-house resource and trainer for the other shifts.

Think again...

Managers of questionable ethics are always on the hunt for freebies and perks, and, since many new pieces of equipment or software packages come with training, this training is a prime target for exploitation.

In my case, I was asked to oversee and operate a new piece of equipment for a small inspection laboratory. It was an unfamiliar device and so I was brought in as having experience with similar devices. I was given equipment manuals and ample time to become comfortable with the system and became productive after a week or so. Of course there are always questions, and I called the manufacturer help line periodically to discuss issues and get answers.

During one of these calls, I was told that my question should have been answered in basic training, at which point I said that I never had any training on their equipment. After searching their database the technician said, yes, they see that a Mr. So-and-so had attended the Basic and Advanced trainings. Now, Mr. So-and-so was my direct boss and he, to my knowledge, never once used the system for any reason, and certainly had never used it to obtain useful results. What he *had* done was to spend two weeks at the manufacturer's new training facility, at his full pay of course, with lunches brought in every day for him and the rest of the students.

It's amusing to me now (but irritating then!) to remember that he never mentioned the training, never offered his services as a tutor, nor did he offer to lend his class materials or notes, if any. I attribute his reticence primarily to the fact that he probably had no intention of running the equipment and therefore paid little attention in class and secondarily to his possible embarrassment should he not be able to run the system properly in my presence.

Why This Works

By being in on the purchase of new equipment or otherwise alert to this sort of opportunity, a manager can act without the knowledge of the employee and without fear of reprisal. He is ready and eager to treat the training as a reward for purchasing the equipment.

The Payoff

As long as the "stolen" perk does not negatively affect the operation sufficiently to draw attention to himself, the manager can relax and enjoy himself. If, in the above example, the training had to be repeated for the actual system operator, the company would have to pay, not the manager directly, so he still wins. To avoid negative repercussions, he may simply blame the operator for not being able to pick up the operation on his own—after all, there are manuals and phone support!

Although a couple weeks of training don't amount to much, even if there is travel to a distant manufacturer's training facility, it does represent an attitude that I find prevalent: Locate the free stuff and take it before someone else does. Forget about what's right, forget about your company's best interests, forget about the efficient use of the equipment you just bought—grab the loot and enjoy it.

And if there's a way to play the supplier salesmen against each other to squeeze out more goodies, then do it. A golf outing, maybe a cruise on the company yacht—what can you negotiate? A good trick that I have personally seen a number of times is to threaten a current supplier by suggesting you are going to switch to his competitor for future business—a *lot* of future business—so he better sweeten the deal or else.

E. D. Everett

Catch Me If You Can

Employees shall have high personal and professional standards of behavior. They must carefully consider the consequences of their actions and decisions, and how these will reflect on the business as a whole. These standards must reflect both corporate and community values.

La la la... I can't *hear* you...

Some people have the right combination of looks, personality and/or skills to retain a position in an organization sometimes for years, even if they have low or nonexistent standards. This scenario seems to be common and I have run across numerous examples of various degrees of severity.

A disconcerting example occurred to me when I was responsible for the creation of the cost sheets for complex quotations, each involving input from several departments. In these quotes, it was the rule that any custom-designed hardware or software had to be purchased by the customer even if the quote was for a lease. In other words, deliverables that were designed and built specifically for a customer would have no value to anyone else, including our company, and so would have to be paid for in full rather than leased. At the end of the lease period, those custom items would be retained by the customer while the leased items were returned to us. Quotes were set up to reflect this directive.

Well, a new young employee was promoted to the position of manager of a key account and shortly thereafter a lease quote was requested for that account. There were a number of custom items included and the cost sheet was set up as per the general directive. After receiving the reviewed quote back for final edits, I noticed that this manager had shifted the non-returnable items into the list of items to be returned at lease end. Confident that this was a simple oversight, I mentioned the error to him while passing in the hallway, saying that we can't structure the quote that way for the reasons stated above. The manager stopped, looked me in the eye without smiling and said, "I can do whatever I want" and walked away. Obviously, he was feeling quite confident and arrogant wielding the power of his new position. If the quote had gone through in that form, the company would have lost a good deal of money on the custom items. However, by making the quote easier for the customer to swallow, this tactic would have resulted in less sales effort for our young gun.

Now, as part of a second similar example, it was also a requirement that each item quoted have a cost, in dollars or hours or both, and each item had to have a source name attached to it in case there were questions or discrepancies during the quote review process. Sometimes during review management would question the figures supplied and call the source in to explain.

One day at a review, numbers from a previously reviewed quote *were* questioned; they seemed too low to cover the deliverable promised. The source was called into the meeting, holding his original documents, and said no, those are *not* the numbers he submitted. Now, assuming a simple mistake of miscopying or transcribing numbers, we looked at the previous version. Hmmm... the numbers in the earlier version are correct. No one at the meeting admitted to changing the spreadsheet, and so the task fell to me to investigate. Luckily, there are limited people who have access to the drive where these sheets are stored, and the software records the user who last made changes and saved the file. Guess who? If you said the same new young manager described above in the first example, you would be correct.

Apparently, he really believed he could do anything he wanted without owning up to it even when, again, it would have cost the company money while filling his pockets if and when we booked the order. Note that he left the source's name attached to the falsified numbers apparently not caring if he, the source, received the third degree. When this thin frame job collapsed, the perpetrator showed no shame or embarrassment—incredible.

In any event, the correct numbers were re-entered and the quote again moved through the review process for final approval.

Another example, although minor, illustrates a similar mindset in a completely different setting. At one of our annual trade shows, our booth management team came up with an incentive designed to encourage the booth staff to engage potential customers and generate leads, those leads being the main takeaway from these events. The staff member who brought in the highest number of leads on each day would receive a cash reward; nothing for second place.

Now generally, I prefer to talk to customers with an actual interest in our products who possess a real potential of benefiting from our solution. The alternative is to get leads for the lead's sake, rather then for a substantial chance to sell product.

But on a slow day to stave off boredom, I decided to go for it and began working booth visitors and passersby strictly to get leads. And at the end of the day I had quite a few more leads than the winner on the previous day, which, in contrast, was a busy one.

When the show closed and the leads were tallied up, my number was announced as the highest not only for the day, but for any daily winner so far. But, wait a minute, one of our young aggressive managers who was also manning the booth then presented his stack of leads and lo and behold he had exactly one more lead than me! And the cash reward was presented to him.

Now, I had been in the booth all day and knew darn well that he had not talked to nearly as many customers as I had. So what had happened? It didn't take long to figure it out. And in the shuttle back to the hotel the "winner" confessed and asked, "Are you mad about what I did?"

He had collected leads from the other booth staff and added them to his until the total just beat mine. I would say the strongest emotion I had at that time was disgust. Here we have a manager who essentially lied about which leads were his, thereby cheating in the contest, then took the money that was not rightfully his. Lying, cheating and stealing—it's the trifecta! I'm sure he's on the fast track up the corporate ladder.

A few days after the show, back at our office, a sales VP, the one who paid out the cash and was in charge of the booth at the time of the event, cornered me in the lobby. This was a brief meeting with just us two. He brought up the lead incident and handed me a gift certificate for the amount of the incentive reward saying, "You deserve it."

Without saying as much, perhaps responding to a rare pang of conscience, he was essentially admitting his knowledge of the deception. But note that he did this only between us two thereby also essentially admitting that our young deceiver will go unexposed and continue to be coddled, protected and rewarded.

You can be quite certain that I never participated in the show lead incentive contests again.

Why This Works

It must be that the lack of ethics and a faulty or absent conscience is quite common—common enough to be accepted and overlooked except in the most grievous circumstances. This would explain the reason why it works: It seems to be the new "normal" and therefore, what's the problem? When you have upper management ignoring or, worse yet, rewarding this behavior it is a strong indication that they, too, do not see anything wrong with it.

The Payoff

Clearly here we are talking raw lust for cash; doing the right thing and playing by the rules must take a back seat to collecting the dough.

Right and Wrong

This organization's key personnel must keep the best interests of their customers, both internal and external, in mind at all times. We count on these key people to do the best they can for a customer and, when things go wrong, as they inevitably sometimes will, stand behind our products and take responsibility for decisions in order to make things right.

Hear no evil, see no evil...

When personal goals take precedence, company goals and normal ethical behavior must take a back seat.

My boss at the time, the account manager for one of our large key customers, received a lead from them for a large order for a new facility for automotive components. The facility was being built as a joint venture between this key domestic customer and a non-key foreign company. My instructions from the boss were to contact the right people at the key company and make sure we were included in the bid process and, once in, do everything we could to ensure the order came our way.

Interestingly, after this initial contact my boss was transferred out of key accounts but, and this is important to understand, still held sales responsibility for non-key customers in the very same area in which this new facility will reside. I, in the meantime, continued my existing sales activity plus took on a share of my now ex-boss' opportunities for this account, of which there were many.

Lo and behold, the ex-boss now declared to the sales VP and our president that since the new project was a joint venture and not a 100% key customer project, it falls under his domain, not mine! And they agreed! And so, control of the sales process for this opportunity was taken away from me.

Ok, shady or not, that's a business decision although I disagree with how it was handled. But that's not the end of the story.

We did end up getting this order, and the systems were installed. Unfortunately, the systems the customer ended up with were too small for their application and would require either replacement or serious modification of each system and software to make them useful—a huge unplanned expense.

Now, as you may have already guessed, our superstar salesman claimed that these systems now *were* part of a key account project and he washed his hands of the whole affair! That's right, in this case of plastic truth and malleable reality, first the order was key, then it wasn't, then it was again.

It was left to me to meet with the irate engineers responsible for the joint venture operation and try to work out a solution that, by the way, cost our company a significant chunk of change. Note that my ex-boss pocketed all the commission for the original order but avoided the responsibility to make it work, while I received nothing but the grief. And stunningly, he offered no apology nor showed any hint of shame or embarrassment, nor even admitted that he could somehow be construed as acting inappropriately. Quite the contrary, he was and is highly regarded in the company both in the U.S. and internationally.

Why This Works

When there is a clique, a good ol' boys network, an "in" crowd that can do no wrong, there is no limit. When you have the powers that be on your side, you are protected. Worse, you are rewarded for this kind of misconduct.

The Payoff

Questionable work, big rewards, no responsibility. It's a dream come true if you have the right personality. Now, I should mention that the salesman described in this incident is very intelligent. He no doubt thought that he was making the right decision at every turn, but certainly the right decision from his perspective only. There is seemingly no limit to the human mind's ability to rationalize.

E. D. Everett

Intended Consequence?

Management must deliberate and carefully weigh the consequences of their decisions to avoid costly mistakes and unintended results. It is more efficient to make a correct decision than to correct a bad one.

But on this planet...

A decision will be made for reasons that, at the time, seem appropriate to the decision-maker. In my experience, a decision in the companies I have worked for has about a 50-50 chance of being the right one. And when it's the wrong one, there is a real good chance that it's a lulu.

Over the course of many years in a particular office building, I had the pleasure of living through multiple remodeling projects including putting up walls, taking them down, replacing old furniture for new and so forth. Over time, I had multiple workspaces including the luxury of having an office with a door, a shared office with one other person, and a group office with three others. I have had cubes of various sizes and descriptions.

During the last remodeling, the decision was made to tear down all office walls and put in nearly identical cubes for everyone, including managers. These were fitted with low walls about four feet high instead of the approximate five foot height of all the previous cube walls.

Now, the height of these walls is such that when seated in your chair you can raise your head and just see across all the walls in the large room. In fact, the cubes are clustered so that the employee's most natural position is facing the corner of two walls. Similarly, unless you were seated at the end of a cluster, three other employees are also facing the same corner that you face. And, if you look up at the right time you stare directly into the eyes of the employee across from you; if you glance to the left or right, there are two other sets of eyes you will likely meet.

If you are lucky, your cube-corner mates are not sick—hacking and coughing and sneezing—because if they are you better stock up on vitamin C, cough and cold medicine, and hand sanitizer.

If your cube-corner mates are on the phone, or talking to someone in person, it's as if they are talking directly at you. If they are all talking at the same time, you better have headphones or have unnatural concentration in order to stay focused. In addition to voices, you can hear the keyboards clicking in the room, drawers opening and closing, the networked copy/fax/scan/printer (it sits out in the open); you can see every action in your visual field from people entering and exiting the room, people standing up or sitting down, deliveries coming and going, etc.

A presumably unforeseen consequence of this layout is that it *encourages* interruption by co-workers. For example, if someone is looking for you and walks in the room, they can see at a glance that you are or are not sitting at your cube, or if you happen to be anywhere else in the room as well. If they pass into your visual field it is likely you will make momentary eye contact. Once that contact is made, even for a split second, the interrupter will smile or nod or point in order to firm up the connection with the interruptee. Once he, the interrupter, feels that a connection is made, he knows he is next in line for your attention.

There is no privacy whatsoever. If you happen to be sitting thinking of the correct wording of, say, an email, your cube-farm mates can easily glance over, notice that you appear to be free and unoccupied, and are thus encouraged to interrupt.

It is interesting to note that managers, including the VPs and president himself, have cubes assigned. This is surprising since so much of their communication is sensitive as it relates to customer problems, employee issues and other matters that shouldn't be discussed in an open group setting. One wonders how this office configuration got approved because, after the remodeling was complete, we see that the managers will routinely take over and park for hours at a time, not at their cube, but in any available conference room. It's only there they can have the privacy they need. The company meanwhile loses the conference rooms as a resource and the managers' cubes sit empty.

Why This Works

I'm sure that every decision has its own circumstances and will not fit easily into a single pattern or mold. Clearly, the decision-maker(s) did not think this one through. The aural and visual din in this sort of mosh pit of phones, voices, and computers is distracting at the very least and, for some, myself included, makes for a high-stress / low productivity environment.

The Payoff

This is one of those topics for which the payoff is hard to pin down. One can only imagine the persons approving the office layout decision do not have to sit in their creation and try to work there. In our case it is true that only our regional office has changed to this design, so the design approver may be ignorant of the mess he has made. On the other hand, maybe the decision maker *is* part of the office team. In this case, he must not admit an error—after all, this was an expensive project in both time and materials.

But whoever signed off on it does get credit for making a decision. See, he's managing! The remodeling is complete, and if he can just hold on a few years, the next remodel may erase his mistake and replace it with another.

E. D. Everett

Conclusion

I have avoided using any examples of misconduct of which I have no personal knowledge. There were certainly rumors of serious malfeasance, some of which, if true, crossed legal and moral boundaries. On the other hand, I have tried to give an honest and accurate account of how business is actually run, using as many examples as possible.

The behaviors described in this writing admittedly don't amount to much in the big picture; we are not talking murder or treason here. But in the aggregate I believe these behaviors and attitudes *do* affect efficiency, productivity and profitability and not just in the infected business. My experience suggests to me that these attitudes are widespread and if they are present in the same ratio in all organizations as those of which I have been part, then businesses across the country are taking a serious hit. At a time when private enterprise is under pressure from increasing regulation at home and from foreign competition, this is exactly what the doctor did *not* order.

It is also quite possible that these behaviors are *expected* to occur and are to be borne just as other costs must be; in aggregate they may be viewed as simply another obstacle to be overcome in the struggle for profit. Perhaps management training includes a session on the cost-to-benefit ratio of dealing with the sort of issues I have raised. It may be cheaper to put up with them than to try to eliminate them.

How does the corruption start?

Imagine you have accepted a position at a company and have met the entire team. They are, to a person, upstanding, honest individuals who try to do the right thing every day, who lead by example, and are shining examples of conduct in the office, in the community, and in their families.

Eventually, the mix will change; it has to. People retire, they die, they move onto other pursuits. At some point a not-so-upstanding person will be introduced. If he is a player or a schmoozer, he will begin to assess the situation, finding out where the weaknesses are, who can be influenced, and how he can manipulate the system and bend it to his advantage.

Once the system is poisoned in this way, it becomes easier for the next bad apple, perhaps an acquaintance of the first, to hire on. And so it goes.

What to do?

There is no single way to answer this question. In my case, after working steadily one way or another since my early teens, starting with paper routes, summer jobs, working through college, and then employed full time for the next 30 years, my solution was to decide to retire as early as possible and remove myself from the day-to-day grind completely.

The trigger for me was my disappointment with the sorry state of management at my last place of employment coupled with seeing incompetence rewarded time and time again. It was made clear that my career had reached its final stage, and rather than put up with any more shenanigans I knew that I *could* control one thing—whether I stayed around for more or left.

Granted that not everyone is in a position to retire, there are other options and maybe better ones at that. First, it is not mandatory that one works for someone else at all: The entrepreneurial type can strike out on his own and create his own business; the artistic can create products in whatever medium such as music, painting, or writing and perhaps find a following; the financial whiz may make his living through investments; and so on. It would be an intimidating choice for me to strike out on my own, but lots of people do it.

An obvious solution is to become "one of them" so-to-speak. Practice your schmoozing skills and use whatever means necessary to get on the good graces of the powers that be and become part of the "in" crowd. Please note that I am not in any way recommending this direction but I have personally seen quite a few people build empires and modest fortunes this way. Still, I would hate to think this book provides inspiration toward that end.

Another option is to try to "fix the system." By this I mean that when an employee witnesses a lapse of ethics or outright criminality, he can become a whistleblower and consequences be damned! To my way of thinking it will take a strong personality and some savings in the bank to be comfortable with this approach, which, I would add, with human nature what it is, will prove to be a losing battle.

Although there are, no doubt, companies out there with management integrity, it seems to me that the temptations are too great, the opportunities too many, for those of the right ilk to take advantage beyond professional limits, and when and where they can take advantage, they will.

For those of you reading this book who are currently employed in corporate America and who have recognized one or more of the scenarios I have laid out—take heart! Know that it's not just you and that it's not unusual. If you remain positive and steadfast you may, hopefully, be able to use this information to your advantage by being aware of what could be happening behind the scenes. When and if you feel you have to make a decision to deal with your particular situation, I hope you will be better equipped to do so.

www.ingramcontent.com/pod-product-compliance
Lightning Source LLC
Chambersburg PA
CBHW060044210326
41520CB00009B/1262